One Day Closer

John M. Burling

Myrtle Beach, SC
November 2014

WESTBOW®
PRESS
A DIVISION OF THOMAS NELSON
& ZONDERVAN

WestBow Press books may be ordered through booksellers or by contacting:

WestBow Press
A Division of Thomas Nelson & Zondervan
1663 Liberty Drive
Bloomington, IN 47403
www.westbowpress.com
1 (866) 928-1240

Cover design by J. M. Burling II

ISBN: 978-1-4908-7685-6 (sc)
ISBN: 978-1-4908-7684-9 (e)

Library of Congress Control Number: 2015905990

Print information available on the last page.

WestBow Press rev. date: 05/06/2015

Contents

Preface

What are we ONE DAY CLOSER to? Everything that will happen in the future. For Christians and those who are particularly students of Biblical Prophesy, they understand that everybody is ONE DAY CLOSER to the second coming of our Lord Jesus Christ. With the changing conditions of the situations in many key countries, it is easier to picture the unfolding events leading up to the second coming. That is not to say that the date is known. Only the Father knows that.

With the downward direction of our country and current unfolding world events and trends, a strong inner urge told the author to get his thoughts documented. This urge was the climax of an interesting set of events. Earlier this year a long time friend invited the author and his wife to attend a Bible study that a group of people from the friend's church had formed. The subject was "Grace" and centered around a book written by Billy Graham's grandson, Tullian Tchividjian, called "One Way Love". We were only able to attend three sessions because of travel plans. After the last session we attended, the author suggested to the friend that an interesting follow up Bible study could be about Biblical Prophesy. The friend agreed. The author has been interested in the subject for some time. While on the trip, the author brought some of his books on the subject along to review in anticipation of the possible Bible study. After returning home and as the author was later watching a news program on TV, a sudden feeling overcame him. In that instant, the author saw the events of the key countries unfold ending in the second coming of Christ. In an immediate second instant, something told the author, that instead of having a Bible study, write a book. Thus "One Day Closer" was born.

In His sermon on the Mount of Olives, Jesus provided the most concise description of the end time. In that sermon He said that, prior to the Flood, people were eating, drinking, marrying and giving in marriage up to the day. Many, maybe most, people today are likewise unaware. The author's prayer is that his family, friends and others will read the book to be aware of what is going on and follow the Chapter 5 comments. The author wants to see them in heaven.

"One Day Closer" is written from the perspective of an engineer and a lay Christian. The Introduction will include the author's experience – military, industry, church and retirement.

Bible quotations are from the New International Version.

Chapter 1

Introduction

An engineer typically brings such disciplines as facts, laws, logic, observations, principles and tenets to understand a situation and/or solve a problem. While not formally trained in the Bible or having a seminary degree, a lay Christian person can pick up knowledge and experience through participating in a variety of church activities over the years and through reading books. The author is a graduate engineer from Purdue University in 1955.

Military/Industrial Experience

After graduation from Purdue, he served his country for two years in the U. S. Army, including fifteen months in Alaska. In the Army, he participated in user tests of Engineer and Armor equipment including: drafting test plans, recording test data and drafting test results. In industry he worked for two firms-Marlin Rockwell Corp. in Jamestown, N. Y., his home town, for six years and for IBM Corp. in five locations for twenty three years. At Marlin Rockwell, a ball-bearing manufacturer, he started as a Time Study Engineer and was promoted to Time Study Manager, responsible for installing and managing the operation of a new standard hour program.

At IBM, he started as an Associate Engineer and was promoted several times, retiring in 1987 at age fifty three as a Senior Engineer. IBM encouraged their employees to further their education. The author then took a course in Simulation where he learned a high level computer language called GPSS. He then met an employee who was a mathematician. They were assigned to create a simulation model of a new manufacturing line. As a result, in the first part of his IBM career, he authored four technical papers on his work creating large scale mathematical/simulation models. The models were used to forecast equipment and manpower requirements for the manufacturing lines and manpower for a large equipment maintenance organization. Appendix D lists the papers.

After, as a Systems Analyst, he serviced inventory, order entry and floor control systems in manufacturing areas. Later, he designed and managed the implementation and operation of new management system for worldwide office products supplies, as Plant Materials Manager. Being the low cost procurement, inventory/warehouse and distribution system in the corporation, it was also used to distribute IBM PC's worldwide and contract shipments of typewriters for a credit card company. He retired in 1987 as Manager of Divisional Marketing Systems.

Church/Stewardship Experience

He was confirmed in the Congregational Church. After marrying Joanne, who he met on a blind date on New Year's Eve, he joined the Lutheran Church in 1960 and has been a member ever since. After their first child was born, Joanne became a stay at home mom. Initially they were occasional church attendees. In 1964, after moving from their home town, he was asked to participate in a stewardship program at their new church. The church attendance picked up then. This started a long association of stewardship of almost fifty years in seven churches, including four as Stewardship Chairman.

He was also elected to Church Council at four churches and Council President at two churches. At two of the churches he was also Finance Committee Chairman at one and Call Committee Chairman at the other. These activities have provided a substantial people interaction and learning process. He has also read most of the Old Testament and all of the New Testament.

In addition, he is an avid reader of Biblical Prophesy books and others including:

Hal Lindsey	The Late Great Planet Earth
	Satan is Alive and Well on Planet Earth
	The Everlasting Hatred The Roots of Jihad
	Faith for Earth's Final hour
Tim LaHaye	Are We living in The End Times?
with Jerry Jenkins	the fictional Left Behind series
David Jeremiah	What in the World is Going On?
Rick Warren	The Purpose Driven Life
	The Purpose Driven Church
Peter Stoner	Science Speaks
Don Piper	90 Minutes in Heaven
Todd Burpo	Heaven is For Real

The prophesy books were well written with significant detail. They were also written by writers with a seminary background. This book will contain references to some of those books. The purpose of this book is to acquaint the reader with both a Biblical perspective and its interactions with history and today's unfolding events. It is written with an engineer's and a lay Christian's perspective.

To many, stewardship is not a popular activity to discuss or be involved with. In fact, many grab their wallet when the subject of stewardship is brought up. The best definition of stewardship the author has heard is: "it is what you do after you say I believe". The three arenas of stewardship are:

1. Personal–what you do for yourself and your family with your time, talent and treasure.
2. Corporate -what you do for others with your time, talent and treasure.
3. Environment how you use it and care for it.

Stewardship starts with the three great commandments of Jesus:

1. Love the Lord your God with all your heart, mind and soul.
2. Love your neighbors as yourself.
3. Go make disciples of all nations.

the prophet Micah added his thoughts:

1. Do justice.
2. Love kindness.
3. Walk humbly before the Lord.

Notice the action words of LOVE, GO, DO and WALK. Time, talent and treasure are three precious gifts given to all by our Lord. As the triangle is the strongest structure form, the church needs members to volunteer their time, talent and treasure. If any of the legs of a triangle are missing, the structure falls. The same is true of the church if any of the church legs are missing. God is the real owner of everything. He created the earth. People on earth only have temporary custody of land, cars, houses and other goods.

In reality, stewardship is involved in all aspects of church life. The three main goals of a Stewardship Committee are:

1. Educate and motivate all members to participate in at least one activity or program beyond worship.
2. Educate and motivate all members to plan a path to tithing their income to the church if they aren't already.
3. Conduct an annual program for members to pledge their time, talent and treasure to their local church.

At a stewardship temple talk, the author challenged the congregation to make a list of their blessings, share them with family and also with others. The author shared his blessings. See Appendix E

Few activities and items are exempt from being measured by someone in some manner. Stewardship is no exception. So, how do you think stewardship is measured? Here is how a form of measurement is referenced by Rick Warren in his mega best seller "The purpose Driven Life", the most profound book the author has read outside of the Bible. Here is a synopsis of page 34 of that book:

"One day you will stand before God and he will do an audit of your life. A final exam before you enter eternity. The Bible says 'remember each of us will stand personally before the judgment seat of God'. From the Bible, we can surmise that God will ask two questions; first, what did you do with my Son Jesus Christ? Did you accept what Jesus did for you and did you learn to love and trust Him? Second, what did you do with your life? —with all the gifts, talents, energy, relationships and resources God gave you? Did you use them for yourself or for the purposes God made you for?"

Each of us can practice the answers to these questions before the real test happens. Now here is an interesting question to ponder. How many years will you spend in eternity compared to the time you will spend on earth? Some people say that our time on earth is like playing an exhibition game. Perhaps it is better to wear out than rust out then.

In Retirement

In retirement, as a snowbird, the author spent ten seasons in Florida working for Caulfield and Wheeler, Inc., a major Civil Engineering firm. There he worked with contractors, developers, agencies and municipalities in costing, obtaining permits, obtaining certifications and obtaining Certificates of Occupancy.

After retirement, the author and his wife became very interested in genealogy and traveling. The author's father was born in Sweden. His mother's parents were born in England. Three of Joanne's grandparents were born in Sweden. The other grandparent had a multi-ethnic background.

To start with, they took a course in genealogy from a Mormon genealogist. In the course, they learned about sources where various records are kept and how to obtain them. Also discussed was a form to record family data on. A few years later, when they got their first computer, they obtained a software program called Family Tree Maker. That system wound up receiving a reservoir of family data as the format was the same as the recording form.

Because a significant part of their family history was in Jamestown, they purchased a second home in the area and returned to their roots. That made them snowbirds, spending six months in Florida and six months in New York. They also rejoined their home church.

Though census and courthouse information, they significantly increased their family history files. In the process, they found many family members in different parts of our country.

Additionally, they traveled to Sweden three times and to England once. In Sweden they met many of the author's family but none of Joanne's as the generation gap was too great. The highlight of their last Sweden trip in 2000 was when a cousin set up a first time family reunion. It was held in the school house the author's father attended through the third grade when he had to quit to work on a farm to help support his family. All four of their children attended the reunion and spent a week together in Sweden. It was the trip of their lifetime.

Joanne has had some success from another effort after joining the Ancestry.Com. Through significant research, she has been able to find her Mayflower connection. She has also been able to tap into others research and find relatives back to the 900's. Genealogy certainly has been an exciting and rewarding hobby.

In retirement, the author continued to write articles and papers for family, friends and local (Jamestown). The titles are listed in Appendix D

After fourteen years of being snowbirds, they have consolidated, sold both houses and live in Myrtle Beach. This was due to an unfortunate medical incident with the author. In 2004 he had a malignant melanoma on the bottom of his foot. After losing half of the foot, the maintenance of two houses was too much. Myrtle Beach was where the family camped several times in the 1970's and 1980's with a group of other IBM families, also retired now. It was an easy decision as three of the families have moved there. The campers have been long retired. The group does B and B trips now.

The Bible (the greatest book ever written)

Documented Biblical Prophesy starts with the Bible. The Bible is authored by forty some different people over a period of two thousand years, starting around four thousand years ago. The writers were each personally inspired by God as what to write. The Bible not only contains prophesy but: the story of Creation; the story of the Flood; books of Law; books of History; books of Poetry; books of the Major Prophets and books of the Minor Prophets in the Old Testament. In the New Testament, the stories continue with the birth, life and death of Jesus Christ in the Gospels; the Letters of Paul; some general Letters and Revelation.

Some people think that the Bible is hokey. We need to pray for them. Facts and logic speak otherwise. First, the Bible is the best selling book of all time, by far. Secondly, it contains a cohesive set of stories by forty some authors over two thousand years. The one common factor was God. Thirdly, an honest assessment of the probability it could have been written by human knowledge is beyond the pale. Fourth, many of the predictions in the Bible have come true. Fifth, countless attempts to refute the Bible have occurred with no success. Jesus himself has fulfilled many prophesy.

One of the profound conclusions by the author about the authenticity of the Bible came from reading a book by Peter Stoner, called "Science Speaks". The book examines the probability of many events described in the Bible as to the probability of pure human knowledge forecasting and describing the event based on the human knowledge of the day. Remember, in 1492 when Columbus discovered America, overwhelming knowledge of the day was that the earth was flat. The evidence accumulated that the Bible must be the truth God wanted us to know.

Chapter 2

Israel, The Focal Point

Overview

Now let's move to this important subject of prophesy. The dictionary defines prophesy as: to tell what will happen; to foretell; to predict. As an overview, there are many keys to understand Biblical Prophesy, fulfillment and the world situation today. In each of these keys God is involved in some manner. He is ultimately in control of all things and events. Only He knows when the end will occur. Through various prophesy in the Bible, many clues have been given about the general time and events in that general time. Through our knowledge of prophesy and understanding and observing how the world events of today are unfolding, we can now see that the general time could be closing more rapidly to the second coming of Jesus Christ. Appendix C contains Matthew 24: 1-44, Jesus' sermon from the Mount of Olives. It is the most concise description of the end of the age.

The Most Obvious Clue

The most obvious prophesy and fulfillment clue came in 1948 when the nation of Israel was formed once more and the Jewish people became a nation again. They had originally been defeated by the Babylonians and their temple, built by Solomon, was destroyed in 586 B. C. They were scattered, mostly to Babylon. When the Babylonians were defeated by the Medes and Persians, many Jews returned to their homeland and started to rebuild their temple, completing it in 516 B. C. The Jewish people were again defeated, this time by the Romans, and their second temple destroyed in 70 A. D. They had then been scattered until 1948.

The point to understand here is that NO other group of people in history that have been defeated and scattered for almost two thousand years have survived as a people, let alone reformed into their own nation in their historic location. Obviously many sub events occurred to make this possible. Now we can cite some Biblical quotes and sub events to explain how God was involved and how it began.

It Started With Abram

First we need to go back four thousand years or so to Abraham's time to see how and why events started as they did and subsequently unfolded. The Bible records how God chose a man named Abram from Ur of the Chaldeans and made a special covenant with him. The purpose of this covenant was to create a special nation to: preserve knowledge of himself; have it as a conduit to reach other people and to provide salvation for all mankind.

Genesis 12: 1-3

Now the Lord said to Abram, "get out of your country, from your father's house to a land that I will show you. I will make you a great nation; I will bless you; and I will make your name great; and you shall be a blessing. I will bless those who bless you; and I will curse those who curse you"

Genesis 12: 6-7

Abram traveled through the land as far as the site of the great tree of Moreh at Shechem. At that time the Canaanites were in the land. The Lord appeared to Abram and said," to your off spring I will give this land". So he built an altar to the Lord who appeared to him.

Genesis 15: 17-19

When the sun had set and darkness had fallen, a smoking firepot with a blazing torch appeared and passed between the pieces. On that day the Lord made a covenant with Abram and said;"To your descendants I give this land from the river of Egypt to the great river Euphrates –the land ofthe Kenites, Kenizzites, Kadmonites, Hittites, Perrizzites, Amorites, Canaanites, Girgashites and Jebusites".

A Family Feud

Now Abram was old and he and his wife Sarai were well beyond child bearing. After ten years, at age eighty six when there was no son, Sarai said to Abram, take Hagar my maid servant. Abram agreed, thinking that they could speed things up. Hagar produced a son who was named Ishmael. Thirteen years later Sarai bore Abram a son named Isaac. As stated in Hal Lindsey's book, "The Everlasting Hatred – The Roots of Jihad", this created a problem as Ishmael was

technically Abram's first born. Then God restated His promise and
changed Abram's name to Abraham.

Genesis 17: 1-8

When Abram was ninety nine, the Lord appeared to him and said;
"I am God Almighty; walk before me blameless. I will confirm
my covenant between me and you and I will greatly increase your
number". Abram fell face down and God said to him; "As for me,
this is my covenant with you; you will be the father of many nations.
No longer will you be Abram; your name will be Abraham, for
I have made you a father of many nations. I will make you very
fruitful; I will make nations of you and kings will come from you.
I will establish my covenant as an everlasting covenant between
me and you and your descendants after you for the generations to
come, to be your God and the God of your descendants after you.
The whole of Canaan, where you are now an alien, I will give as an
everlasting possession to you and your descendants after you; and I
will be their God".

Genesis 17: 15-22

God said to Abraham, "As for Sarai your wife, you are no longer
to call her Sarai; her name will be Sarah. I will bless her so that she
will be the mother of nations; kings of peoples will come from her".
Abraham fell face down; he laughed and said to himself, 'will Sarah
bear a child at the age of ninety'? and Abraham said to God; "if only
Ishmael might live under your blessing". Then God said "yes,but
your wife Sarah will bear you a son and you will call him Isaac. I will
establish my covenant with him as an everlasting covenant for his
descendants after him. And as for Ishmael, I have heard you. I will
surely bless him; I will make him fruitful and will greatly increase his
numbers. He will be the father of twelve rulers and I will make him
a great nation. But my covenant I will establish with Isaac, whom

Sarah will bear to you by this time next year". When he had finished speaking with Abraham, God went up from him.

The preceding passages caused the start of a long and continuous family feud. The descendants of Ishmael contend that he was the first born and intended heir. We will see as the book unfolds. Ishmael's descendants eventually became Arabs and Islamics. This feud has been kept alive through history with some periods of hostility toward the Jewish people in their scattered locations. It particularly escalated to violence after Mohammed came on to the scene in 590 A. D. According to Islam, in 610 A. D. Mohammed received a revelation from a messenger from God. From that revelation, Mohammed believed he was sent to reestablish monotheism as it had originally been revealed. he believed the original recipients, Christians and Jews, had corrupted God's true revelation. This is the fundamental belief that guaranteed a large collision with Christians and Jews. It is a collision that cannot be settled other than by God.

The following quote is from Hal Lindsey's book on the claim on Jerusalem. "It is vital to recognize the name Jerusalem never appears in the Koran. The claim to this city arose years after Mohammed's death. The justification comes from a verse which says Mohammed traveled to the utter most mosque (which is the meaning of Al Quds in Arabic) shortly before his death. The legend continues that Mohammed, escorted by the angel Michael, flew on a winged horse named Barak of the Temple Mound to Jerusalem. As the story goes, Mohammed ascended to the seventh heaven from the great rock and flew back to Mecca. Omar was the first to erect a mosque over the sacred site. A more magnificent mosque was later built there —the Dome of the Rock. No historical evidence shows Mohammed was ever in Jerusalem. But in the Middle East it doesn't matter whether something is actually true. What is believed to be true is all that matters. Many have died for the sake of myths".

The Temple Mound is the location where Solomon's temple and the second temple were built and destroyed. Now that Israel is a nation and in possession of the land, activities to build a third temple, as prophesied, are being planned. The Temple Mound is the third holiest place of Islam after Mecca and Medina. Does this situation look like a collision of an irresistible force meeting an immovable object? This has now spilled into a world problem. As a law of physics states, two objects of matter cannot occupy the same space. This in a nutshell is the problem stated. Only God will be able to solve it at the second coming of Jesus Christ.

A Bible Summary

We can now fill in the next part of the story with a summary of events and Biblical quotes that lead up to the birth, life and death of Jesus Christ and the last book in the Bible, Revelation. Isaac had a son named Jacob who had several sons, one named Joseph. Apparently Joseph was a favorite. His brothers were jealous and sold him to Ishmaelites at age seventeen. They took Joseph to Egypt. There they sold him to one of Pharaoh's officials. The official found favor with Joseph and put him in charge of his household. Through his wife falsely accusing him, Joseph was put in prison. Joseph, then through the Lord, interpreted dreams of two prisoners which came true. When Pharaoh heard of this, he asked Joseph to interpret his dream.

Joseph told of seven years of plenty and seven years of famine. Goods were then put aside and Joseph was eventually put in charge of all Egypt. When the famine hit, Egypt had plenty but Canaan had a famine. Ten of Jacob's sons went to Egypt to buy grain. Eventually, the brothers recognized Joseph as their brother. Jacob's whole family and many others were then invited to Egypt to escape the famine. They prospered and grew while Joseph was in charge. After Joseph died in 1805 B. C., there was a gradual disfavor of the Israelites. Eventually they became slaves for many years. Because the Israelites were multiplying, Pharaoh ordered all males be killed, but girls could live. A boy was born to a Levite couple. After three months, the mother put the child in a reed basket, coated it with pitch and tar, and placed it along the bank of the Nile. Pharaoh's daughter discovered it. She felt sorry for the boy. After finding the mother, Pharaoh's daughter asked the mother to nurse the baby for her. She named him Moses since he was drawn from water.

Moses grew. One day he went out to see his own people. An Egyptian was beating one of his own people. Moses killed the Egyptian. When Pharaoh heard about this, he ordered Moses killed. Moses then fled. Eventually the Pharaoh died. Meanwhile, the Lord heard the cries of his people in bondage. Remembering his covenant with the Hebrews, he called on Moses. After convincing Moses that God was with him, Moses asked to let his people go. Pharaoh refused. Many plagues were then put on the Egyptian people: of blood; of Frogs; of flies; of Gnats; on livestock; a Hadj of darkness and finally killing the first born of Egyptians.

The Lord informed Moses and his brother Aaron on the tenth of the month each family is to take a lamb. On the fourteenth day they are to slaughter the lambs at midnight and take the blood and put it on the sides, tops and door frames of their houses. Then they must roast the lamb and not leave any until morning. If any is left, it needs to be burned. The Lord said; "eat it in haste. It is the Lords Passover. On that same night, I will pass through Egypt and strike every first born —both men and animals —and I will bring judgment on the gods of Egypt. I am the Lord. The blood will be a sign for you on the houses where you are; and when I see the blood, I will pass over you. No destructive plague will strike you".

The Hebrews did as they were told. The Lord did as He said He would. Pharaoh finally relented and gave the Hebrews supply and treasure for their journey. After the Hebrews left, numbered in the thousands, the Lord hardened Pharaoh's heart. Pharaoh suddenly learned that Egypt had lost treasure and their slaves. He organized his army for pursuing the Hebrews. The Hebrews had made it to the edge of the Nile. Pharaoh's army was closing in.

Then the Lord said to Moses, "Why are you crying out to me? Tell the Hebrews to move on. Raise your staff and stretch your hand over the sea to divide the water so that the Hebrews can go through the sea on dry ground. I will harden the hearts of the Egyptians so they go after them".

Moses did what the Lord bade. The Hebrews went through the sea to the other side on dry ground. The Egyptians pursued them. The Lord then bade Moses to raise his staff and stretch his hand again. Moses did and the sea went back to its place. It covered the Egyptians. There were no survivors.

The Hebrews roamed the desert area for forty years before they reached Canaan again. During that period they complained about many things. The Lord provided manna for them to eat. They also built idols. Eventually the Lord called Moses to Mount Sinai where he gave Moses The Ten Commandments. The Hebrews grew in population but for hundreds of years it was a chaotic time. Things settled down under the kingships of Saul, David and Solomon. Solomon succeeded in building their temple. In the eighth to sixth centuries B. C., the Major Prophets predicted the fall of the kingdom, the scattering of the people, a later restoration of the kingdom and of the Lord's Son, Jesus Christ.

Isaiah 1 – A Rebellious People

Isaiah 2 – The mountain of Love, The day of the Lord

Isaiah 3 – Judgment on Jerusalem

Isaiah 7: 13-14

Then Isaiah said, "Hear now you house of David. Is it not enough to try the patience of men? Will you try the patience of my God also? Therefore the Lord himself will give you a sign. The virgin will be with child and give birth to a son and will call him Immanuel".

Isaiah 11: 10-12

"In that day the root of Jesse will stand as a banner for the people, the nations will rally to Him and His place of rest will be glorious. In that day, the Lord will reach out His hand a second time to claim the remnant that is left of His people from Assyria, from lower Egypt, from upper Egypt, from Cush, from Elam, from Babylon and from the islands of the sea. He will raise a banner from the nations and gather the exiles of Israel; he will assemble the scattered of Judah from the four corners of the earth".

Jeremiah 25: 1-5 Seventy years of captivity

Jeremiah 30, 31 Restoration of Israel

Ezekiel 1-24 He began six years before the destruction of Jerusalem with his prophesies and kept on predicting its destruction until it happened.

Judah was in fact destroyed by the Babylonians along with their temple in 586 B. C. They were scattered, some to Babylon and some to other places in the region. They returned gradually to their homeland around 535 B.C. and rebuilt their temple by 516 B. C. as predicted. The Babylonians had been defeated. The victors, Medes and Persians, allowed the Judeans to return over many years.

Meanwhile, another significant prophet, Daniel appeared. He was one of the Judeans captured and taken to Babylon. Daniel and some of his friends of royalty were selected for their wisdom to enter into the king's service. The king found them significantly better than all his magician and enchanters. At some point later, the king had a troubled dream he did not understand. The king asked his astrologers to interpret the dream. They could not. The king then ordered them killed.

Daniel found out about the king's dream. During that night, Daniel had a dream that was revealed to him by the Lord. Daniel then went to Arioch where the astrologers were held. He told the guards he could interpret the dream. He was then taken to the king. Daniel then told the king about the dream."The picture you saw is a great image whose form was awesome. Its head was of fine gold, its chest and arms of silver, its belly and thighs of bronze and it feet partly of iron and partly of clay. You watched while a stone was cut without hands, which struck the image on its feet of iron and clay broke into pieces. Then the iron, the clay, the bronze,the silver and gold were crushed together and became chaff like which blew away. The stone became a great mountain and filled the whole earth. This is the dream".

Daniel then told the king of the interpretation. "The image's head of gold was you. God has given you a kingdom and power to rule all. After your kingdom another kingdom will rise, inferior to yours, the chest and arms of silver. Then a third kingdom will rise, the belly and thighs of bronze and shall rule all. A fourth kingdom will rise and will be as strong as iron but shatter into pieces. That kingdom will crush all others. Since you saw the toes of iron and clay, the kingdom will be divided and will be partly strong and partly weak.

As you saw, iron and clay will not adhere. God has made known to the king what will pass after this. The dream is certain and its interpretation is sure".

Five hundred years later the prophesy was fulfilled exactly as Daniel had prophesied. Babylon was the first kingdom. The Medes and Persians followed. The Greeks under Alexander were next. Rome was the fourth kingdom, which felled Judea in 70 A. D. and destroyed the second temple. When Alexander died, his generals divided the empire into four kingdoms. The kingdoms were eventually absorbed by Rome. While Rome is no longer an empire today, most Western nations have taken their basic principles of government from Rome i.e. laws, statutes, senate, etc. Daniel also revealed another dream later to the king. He described ten future kings that will not always get along with the leader. Three will rebel and be crushed.

Daniel 7: 19-20

"I wished to know the truth about the fourth beast, which was different from all others, exceedingly dreadful with the teeth of iron and its nails of bronze which devoured, broke into pieces and trampled the residue with its feet and about the ten horns that were about his head which came up before three fell, namely the horn which had eyes and a mouth that spoke pompous words, whose appearance was greater than his fellows".

Daniel 7: 24

"The ten horns are ten kings who shall rise after them; he shall be different from the first ones, and shall subdue three kings".

Fast forward briefly. After World War One, there was a clamor for "peace in our time". At a conference of nations in Greece, the agreement of a one world government was established, called The

League of Nations. Many countries adopted it but not the United States. After World War Two, many nations met again and The United Nations was founded. This time the United States joined. The world headquarters is in New York City. Years later, many European countries formed the European Union, another step toward the consolidation of a one world government.

The Hebrews started to return to their land in 538 B. C. after the Medes and Persians had defeated the Babylonians. The last group had started to return by 432 B. C. Meanwhile, the prophets Micah and Zachariah had prophesied a new ruler over Israel.

Micah 5:2

"But you Bethlehem Ephrathah, through you are small among the clans of Judah, out of you will come one who will be ruler over Israel whose origins are from old, from ancient times".

Zachariah 9:9

"Rejoice greatly O Daughters of Jerusalem! See, your king comes to you, righteous and having salvation, gentle and riding on a donkey".

The birth, life and death of Jesus Christ is told in the Gospels by Jesus' disciples, Matthew, Mark, Luke and John. After the death and resurrection of Christ, the book of Acts described initial activities in the start of the church. Paul's letters to the many churches followed as well as the other general letters. The last book of the Bible, Revelation, was written by the disciple John, who was in his nineties and a prisoner on Patmos Island.

Chapter 3
The World Situation

The Players

The six key players in the world today are: Israel, Iran, Russia, United States, China and Africa. The following is only a brief history of each country/land, highlighting major interactions and conflicts. It is intended to lead up to why and what is currently happening that could possibly bring on the second coming more rapidly. Understanding what is going on in these countries and their interactions is key to understanding the unfolding world events.

Israel

Now for the rest of the story of Israel becoming a nation again. The Jewish people were scattered again after their defeat by the Romans and the second temple destroyed in 70 A. D. This scattering lasted until the end of World War One when the Jewish people started to return to their land in larger numbers. Years before, the Ottoman Empire captured and controlled the Middle East along with large portions of Eastern Europe and Asia for centuries. The land of Canaan became almost barren. Slowly some Jews trickled back and started to cultivate the land to some extent. Seeing employment opportunities, Arabs also trickled in and the population of both Jews and Arabs slowly grew over time.

Some interesting events around World War One led to the start of the eventual state of Israel in 1948. In the war, the English armies used cordite to produce gunpowder. A chemical to produce cordite had to be imported from Germany. The English government found a chemist named Chiam Weizmann. He developed a process to produce synthetic acetone, which is used in to produce cordite. It was a significant help in the victory over Germany. This earned favor with the English government. He then petitioned that government for a Jewish state. In the war, England gained possession of Palestine. What resulted was the Balfour Declaration which states that England favors a homeland for the Jewish people.

The League of Nations was also in agreement and gave England authority over the whole Middle East. The Middle East was then carved up into several countries; Iran, Iraq, Turkey, Palestine and others. Apparently some in England then decided on appeasing the Arabs and gave eighty percent of the original Jewish mandate to the Arabs. The new territory of Palestine continued under English protection through and after World War Two.

After World War Two, there were local conflicts between the Jews and Arabs. England finally relented and agreed to a state of Israel. At the same time the country of Jordan was formed, partly from Palestine. On May 14, 1948 the state of Israel was finally created. Almost immediately, U. S. President Harry Truman recognized Israel. They had finally reformed into their own nation after almost two thousand years. Jews from other countries and the remnant of the World War Two holocaust started to flow into Israel.

Israel today is the only ally of U. S. in the Middle East. U. S. has been Israel's friend and supporter since its reestablishment. Since its reestablishment, Israel has been in a perpetual state of war with terrorists in surrounding countries. Despite these events, the country has grown and become wealthy. Israel's population is about six million people. It is surrounded by countries of around three hundred million people who want to wipe Israel off the map. It is a mismatch. In order to defend herself, she is armed to the teeth. She also has the Samson option to exercise if defeat is imminent. She has been in two major wars with her neighbors, who were supported by USSR, now Russia. Against overwhelming odds, she was able to win both the Six Day War and the Yom Kipper attack. Some speculate divine help was involved. As you may know, Israel is a small country, about the size of New Jersey. At one point, she is barely ten miles wide.

The current U. S. president, Barak Obama, has appeared to soften the support of Israel with his rhetoric and actions, more favoring the Arabs. He has openly criticized Israel while praising the Arabs. He has also kept a hands off policy of getting involved with conflicts in the area under his watch. In addition, he has talked about downsizing the military to pre- World War Two levels. This has embolden Israel's enemies, including Russia and Iran to encourage their surrogates, the Islamic terrorists.

It is well to remember what God promised Abraham many centuries ago. "I will bless those who bless you and will curse those who curse you." For many centuries England was a world power. There was an expression that said "the sun never sets on England." Today England is a shell of its once proud territories. Could it be that God had a hand in that? Beware U. S.

Iran

Iran (Persia) has been a continuous state going back to Biblical times. The Medes and Persians were the second world power that Daniel dreamed about, the chest and arms of silver. After, they were captured by Alexander and the Greeks and later they were also part of the conquest of Genghis Khan and still later part of the Ottoman Empire. When the Ottoman Empire was part of the defeated in World War One, the country of Iran was established.

Over the early years, Iran was relatively docile until oil was discovered there. Iran then became more modernized and developed. In the 1970's the Shah of Iran was the Islamic ruler. He was a good ally of U. S. in the area. In the late 1970's the Shah needed to go to U. S. for some medical work. At the same time, the U. S. president, Jimmy Carter, talked about some human rights atrocities the Shah participated in, in Iran. While the Shah was in U. S., this emboldened some radicals in Iran. They took over the country then. At the same time, the radicals detained the U. S. ambassador and his contingent for over a year. Many people still talk about the failed U. S. rescue attempt when two U. S. helicopters collided in the Iranian desert.

With the new U. S. President, Ronald Reagan, the terrorists released the hostages as they were fearful of retaliation. The radical Ayatollah Khomeini then became the leader of Iran. Relations with both U. S. and Israel worsened and continue to do so today. While many Iranians are open to living with more freedoms, Iran is an oppressive country with those citizens. Iran is also part of radical Islam bent on the destruction of Israel. Today they are the main funder of radicals in other areas also.

For some time, Iran has been working on enriching uranium. U. S. and most of the free world are concerned that the enrichment will lead to the development of atomic weapons. Already Iran has missile capability of reaching Israel and perhaps beyond. Iran says they are enriching to develop power. That is suspicious as Iran has a glut of its own oil and could easily use it for power. Some economic sanctions have been imposed on Iran by the U. S. and the United Nations. Talks continue and so does the enrichment process. President George W. Bush labeled Iran one of the three countries a part of the axis of evil. End time prophesy says that Russia and Iran will join forces and attack Israel. Iran is well on their way to participate in such a venture.

Russia

For centuries Russia was a poor country and almost forgotten on the world stage. In the late 1700's, Peter the Great tried to bring the people and massive country to a more modern state, with little results. It still remained a repressive country and relatively primitive. It suffered defeat in the Russo Japanese War in 1905. During World War One, the people overthrew the tsar, executed his family, ending the monarchy for good. Since then the Russian people have remained repressed with the communist dictators eliminating millions of people.

When Hitler and the Germans disregarded their non-aggression pact and invaded Russia in 1941, Russia had no choice other than to defend themselves and defeat Hitler. The U. S. provided a large amount of war material and food to Russia to aid them in the effort. The Russians paid a huge price during the war, losing millions of people, many cities and much infrastructure.

After the European conflict ended in May, 1945, Germany was divided up between U. S., England, France and Russia. Berlin, the capital, was in the Russian zone. It was separately divided by the above countries. The U. S., England and France divisions became West Germany. The Russian sector became East Germany.

Russia kept most of their military personnel and equipment in their zone. The other countries kept little personnel and equipment except U. S. who kept a large force but less than Russia. Russia kept their zone under tight control with very little rebuilding. On the other hand, the Western zone was given food. Significant U. S. aid was involved with economic recovery and rebuilding. Russia closed assess to Berlin through their zone. An air lift led by U. S. provided for their Berlin section for some time.

These tensions continued to grow into what was dubbed the Cold War. The first major confrontation was in 1962 when it was discovered that Russia was building missile sites in Cuba, ninety miles from U.S. President Kennedy ordered a blockade of Cuba and Russian ships stopped and searched for missile parts and supplies. Fortunately the Russians backed down and the situation ended peacefully. Russia disbanded the missiles and sites.

The tension continued however. In the 1980's, U. S. had started a missile shield program called Star Wars under President Reagan. The Russians also started a comparable program but with all the spending, became almost bankrupt. They then elected a more moderate leader and tensions eased with U. S. In the process, Russia lost all of the countries and territories she annexed after World War Two. Interestingly, President Reagan in 1988 admonished the Russian President to tear down the Berlin Wall. With lessening security at the wall, the natives tore the wall down in 1989. The two Germanys then united and grew to have a strong economy.

In the early 2000's tensions started to increase between U. S. and Russia. Russia had elected a former KGB (secret police) member, Vladimir Putin. After electing a puppet of Putin, he was reelected.

Putin had started to rebuild the military. Many people in the know, believe that he has dreams of reconstituting the former territories, now independent countries, and more.

Earlier in 2014, Russia stirred up former Russian citizens in Ukraine to protest for annexation to Russia. They were backed up by Russian troops invading Crimea, a part of Ukraine. A "vote" was taken and Crimea is now part of Russia. In July, 2014, other separatists shot down Ukraine cargo planes and a Malaysian commercial aircraft, killing three hundred passengers and crew. With a possible demilitarization of U. S. under President Obama, the stage could be set for closing in on the end times.

United States

After Columbus' trips to America, Northern America started to slowly have Europeans trickle in in the1500's. It started to become colonized by primarily England, France and Spain in the 1600's. The Dutch, Sweden and others were also involved but in smaller numbers. Through various conflicts, England became the prominent controller of territory. The king of England was, therefore, the ruler of North America.

The people who came to North America from the European countries were looking for freedom and opportunities for a better life. Although pioneer life was very difficult, the pioneers were a very hardy and persistent people. They were also very freedom loving and God fearing. As the country grew, local government and legislative acts grew. The king became very annoyed with these local acts and enacted some punitive responses. One such response was to add a huge tax on tea, a favorite beverage of both the home country and the colonists. The colonists revolted and boarded a ship, loaded with a new tea shipment, in the Boston Harbor in the night dressed as

Indians. The tea aboard the ship was dumped into the harbor. The event was dubbed "The Boston Tea Party".

Other incidents started throughout the colonies and escalated. The climax was when, in 1774, a group of colonists fired on a group on English soldiers (redcoats). This escalated into a full blown war, known as the Revolutionary War. Most initial battles were won by the redcoats. The colonists, under George Washington and other courageous leaders, eventually turned the tide and defeated the English General Cornwallis at Yorktown, Virginia in 1781.

The colonists then set about forming a government. By that time the thirteen colonies had their own form of a state and local government. The formal revolt had started earlier with a document by Thomas Jefferson called the Declaration of Independence, declaring the colonists intention. It was dated July 4, 1776, which U. S. has referred to as Independence Day, heartily celebrated every year. The Declaration was signed by fifty six leaders of the thirteen colonies. See Appendix A

The process to form a required national government was a messy one. A big fear of all the states was that of an all powerful federal government. The states remembered the English king and his one man rule. Finally in 1782, a constitution was drafted by James Madison of Virginia, eventually agreed to, and signed by representatives from each state. It was then ratified by state legislators. The Constitution of the United States is THE governing document of U. S. It states the role and restrictions given to the federal government by the states. Where not specified, the states would have the role. Initially, ten amendments were approved, known as the Bill of Rights, for other restrictions on the federal government. Over the next two hundred years, the Constitution has been amended seventeen more times.

The two biggest influences in creating the Constitution were the English Magna Charta and the colonists Judeo-Christian beliefs. The Constitution is the greatest document man ever created that describes how ruling by the people works. George Washington was the first president of the United States. See Appendix B

England was not finished with warfare against the U. S. In the 1810's another war with England occurred. They captured Washington D. C., the capital, and burned the White House and legislative buildings. U. S. finally defeated England for good, culminating in a battle on Lake Erie in 1812. After, relations with England improved to where they eventually became one of the U. S. greatest allies.

The U. S. started to grow, migrating west and south. States and territories were added. By the 1850's, the country was coming to a boiling point. Of course the Constitution and Declaration of Independence were against slavery. Africans blacks were kidnapped by slave traders over many years and brought to U. S. and other countries and sold as slave labor. The South U. S. used them as legal slaves. The North U. S. had no such laws. The conflict erupted into the Civil War, starting in Charleston, S. C. in 1861. It was the worst chapter in U. S. history. Hundreds of thousands of soldiers and citizens were killed. The north finally won with General Grant defeating General Lee at Appomattox Court House, Virginia in 1865. Many cities and what infrastructure there was, was ravaged. President Lincoln had both freed the slaves and saved the union in the process.

The reconstruction took many years. During the reconstruction, the country both expanded territory and started to become industrialized. By the end of the century, the U. S. was one of the strongest economic and military powers. There were ups and downs along the way. In 1898, there was a short war with Spain. A U. S. warship docked in Cuba was sunk. In defeat, Spain lost possessions of Cuba, the Philippine Islands and other lesser territories. Shortly after, the U. S. gave Cuba their independence. The Philippines received their independence after World War Two.

The U. S. continued to grow and industrialize as the twentieth century unfolded. In 1914, the Archduke of Serbia was assassinated by a person from Hungary. This event triggered World War One as countries on each side had treaties that required support of friends. Germany, Hungary and Turkey were on one side and England and France were on the other side. Turkey was part of the Ottoman Empire which controlled Eastern Europe and the Middle East. The war was almost a stalemate in France, the major battlefield. U. S. at first, through President Wilson, tried to be neutral. The Germans wound up sinking a U. S. passenger ship, the Lusitania with a submarine. This and other incidents brought U. S. into the conflict. With U. S. military support, the Germans finally surrendered, ending the war in 1918. As part of the victory, the Ottoman Empire was dismantled into several countries/territories, Palestine being one such territory.

The U. S. continued to boom through the "Roaring Twenties" until 1929 under President Hoover. The stock market collapsed, unemployment soared and the country reeled. The recovery was slow under President Roosevelt through 1939. At that time, a reconstituted Germany started World War Two by invading Poland. England and France teamed again. In 1940, Germany defeated their armies on French soil. With luck and guts, England saved much of their military with a huge evacuation at Dunkirk, France. The evacuation used every military, commercial and private boat available, braving submarine infested waters.

The U. S. did not enter the war immediately. They did, however, through a lend lease program, provide ships and food to England. It was a precarious process traveling through submarine infested waters. Finally the U. S. declared war on the Japanese because of an attack on the naval base at Pearl Harbor, Hawaii on December 7, 1941. A few days later, U. S. declared war on Germany and the Axis Nations because of several incidents.

It was a bloody war with almost a half million U. S. casualties. Many memorial events occurred in the Pacific: the Doolittle raid on Tokyo; Battle of Midway; Bataan and Corregidor; Guadalcanal; the Solomon Islands; Gilbert and Marshall Islands; Tarawa; the Great Marianas Turkey Shoot; the Philippines; Iwo Jima; and Okinawa to name some.

The overwhelming industrial might of the U. S. was a significant factor in the defeat of Japan. In addition, the development of the atomic bomb was the final blow to Japan. Two atomic bombs were dropped, one on Hiroshima and one on Nagasaki, with horrendous effects. Japan almost immediately surrendered, saving countless lives if an invasion of Japan was done. The peace ceremony was held on September 2, 1945 on the battleship Missouri in Tokyo Bay

The concurrent battlefield in Europe was ended earlier on May 2, 1945. The U. S. entry in the war was initially a supply role, building up both air and ground forces in England. The air war was started in 1942 and continued until the end of the war. Long range U. S. and English bombers created a devastating effect on Germany. The ground war started in 1943 in Africa, taking back territory gradually from the Germans and their allies, Italy and Rumania. Memorable events were: Kasserine Pass; Benghazi; Tobruk; and El Alamein in Africa. Next came the Italian campaign which included: Sicily; Salerno; Anzio; Monte Cassino and Rome. Italy surrendered in 1944, but the Germans in Italy hung on until the end of the war.

Meanwhile another effort had been in process, the retaking of France and Germany from the west. A huge buildup of men, materials and aircraft had accumulated in England under General Dwight Eisenhower. The largest land invasion in history, Operation Overlord, then occurred. Tens of thousands of troops and supporting equipment landed on the French coast on June 6, 1944, known as D-Day. Paratroopers had landed in earlier in the night. Ships bombarded the landing zones. Aircraft bombed and strafed the landing areas and beyond.

It was a successful landing. The allied forces of U. S., England, France and others secured the beachhead and gradually moved inland. Memorable battle sites included: the beaches of Omaha, Juno, Gold and Sword; Cherbourg; St. Lo; Point Du Hoc; the hedge rows; Paris; Arnhem; Bastogne; Ramagen Bridge ; crossing the Rhine and finally meeting up with the Russian troops from the east. Berlin fell, Hitler committed suicide and Germany surrendered on May 2, 1945.

The U. S. kept an occupying force in Germany. Through the Marshall Plan, U. S. provided a significant assistance to help rebuild after the war. Soon West Germany became self governed with elections and a new constitution. The U. S. occupying role diminished to a defensive role and keeping a contingent group of troops, equipment and aircraft in Germany to this day. Relations with Germany migrated to becoming allies and remain so. With the collapse of the Berlin Wall and Russia's diminished role in Germany, East and West Germany have become one nation. Gradually the East has been rebuilt. The German economy has grown to be the strongest in Europe. The U. S. also kept an occupying force in Japan and a similar situation occurred with the Japanese economy boom and becoming a good ally.

Then in June 1950, North Korea, a surrogate of China, invaded South Korea, a friend of U. S. and also a growing economic country. President Truman authorized a response and General McArthur,

U. S commander in Japan, took the lead. The war seesawed for a while, but South Korea, with U. S. help, eventually pushed back the North Koreans and a truce was agreed to but never signed. Relations between the two Koreas remain tense, even today. A contingent of U. S. military remains stationed in South Korea today.

In the early 1960's, intelligence reports indicated the communists in Vietnam, supported by China, were encroaching from the north for a possible takeover of that country. Under the domino theory, President Kennedy sent U. S. advisors to Vietnam. Skirmishes escalated and President Johnson sent U. S. troops, equipment and aircraft to stop the takeover. It wound up a stalemate and a guerilla type war. The U. S. public grew fed up with the loss of life. With a new election, President Nixon eventually saved some face and brought the troops home. It was a very divisive time in U. S.

The Cuban missile crisis occurred in 1962. See the Russia section for details. Earlier, President Kennedy used authorized U. S. support for Cuban exiles to take back their country from Fidel Castro, the Cuban dictator. It ended up a disaster for the exiles and Castro remains in control today, with his brother, Raul.

U. S. and Russia were engaged in a technical duel about space exploration. Russia was first putting a man in space, circling the earth in 1957. President Kennedy, in 1960, challenged the space program and country to put a man on the moon by the end of the decade. The U. S. space program had started but lagged the Russians. It was a proud accomplishment when U. S. did put a man on the moon in 1969. The space program continued strong until 2008, when President Obama decided to stop any further manned space exploration. U. S. did participate with Russia in a permanent space station. The only way to the space station now is aboard a Russian vehicle.

In the 1990's Saddam Hussein, dictator of Iraq, attacked neighbor Kuwait with eyes past Kuwait. President George H. W. Bush responded quickly. After U. N. approval, U. S. and a group of nation quickly removed the Iraqi troops and Kuwait was restored. Many thought the force should have gone to Bagdad, and ousted the dictator, but the U. N. resolution did not call for that.

In 2001 tragedy struck the U. S. Islamic terrorists, on 9-11-01, hijacked four U. S. domestic airline flights within minutes of each other, took over the cockpit and rerouted the aircraft to other destinations. Two of the aircraft went to New York City and each hit one of the twin towers of the World Trade Center. The towers fell in short order, killing almost three thousand people. Many brave firefighters and police lost their lives in attempting rescues. A third plane was rerouted to Washington, D. C. and struck the Pentagon, killing many there. The forth aircraft was rerouted and headed east. By that time, passengers, through cell phone contacts, found out about the other three aircraft. Some brave passengers assaulted the cockpit. The aircraft crashed out control harmlessly in a field near Shanksville, Pennsylvania

Intelligence found that Afghanistan was the main training ground for the terrorists. George W. Bush quickly mobilized the military and then quickly struck the known bases. Afghanistan is a rugged mountainous country with a limited central government, mostly ruled by local tribal chiefs. The Russians learned their lesson trying to conquer it, finally leaving after big losses. Through partnering with the local tribes, a lot of the terrorists were eliminated. The U. S. then got bogged down trying to find the leader, Osama Bin Laden, and to do nation building. President Obama is now in the process of disengaging.

Saddam Hussein, through U. S. and other intelligence, was believed to be working to develop nuclear and other weapons of mass destruction. With Iraq's refusal of international inspections, the U. N. authorized the use of force. The U. S., with a coalition of nations, defeated the Iraqi army in short order. Saddam escaped but was eventually found, put on trial by the Iraqi people, and executed. Meanwhile the U. S. led a nation building effort. It is hard to build a democracy in short order. Elections were held and a fragile government was in place. The new president, Barak Obama, campaigned on getting the troops out of Iraq. He succeeded but left the fragile democracy go it on their own. The Navy Seals finally found Osama Bin Laden hiding in Pakistan. With a daring raid he was captured and killed by the Seals.

In 2012 the U. S. embassy in Benghazi, Libya was assaulted by terrorists. The ambassador, two Navy Seals, and a guard were killed. The investigation into it is still in process. Also in 2012 a war broke out in Syria between the Syrian army and a group seeking to overthrow the president. It involved some use of poisonous gas. President Obama issued a red line ultimatum if used again, then backed down when the Russian president took over and negotiated the destruction of the gas. Soon after, another Islamic terror group, ISIS, formed and attacked Iraq. Iraq was not able to stop the group, who now controls about one third of Iraq. The group is also imposing Sharia law on the captured area. That is the situation at book time.

China

Please see The Finale section.

Africa

Please see The Finale section.

Chapter 4

End Time Prophesy

The Role of America

The role of America in end time prophesy is not mentioned in the Bible. Prophesy scholars are puzzled and can only speculate about why. U. S. was founded on Judeo-Christian principles. Throughout its short history it has been a force for good. Of course it has had some sins. All people sin and fall short of the glory of God. Countries sin also. But U. S. has gotten past the sins of slavery and Indian treatment. It has launched the world's greatest missionary movement. It has been a beacon of freedom. It has also been a leader standing up to despots as well as significantly helping to rebuild damage caused by the despots. God has certainly blessed the U. S. in many ways, both in its founding and its short history.

In his book, "What in the World is Going On?", Dr. David Jeremiah speculated about three possible explanations as to why the role of U. S. is not mentioned in the Bible:

1. America will be incorporated into the European Coalition

2. America will be invaded by outside forces
3. America will be infected by moral decay

In the author's opinion, sadly the highest probability is that America will be infected by moral decay which will render her helpless or unwilling or both. Let's look at some facts about what is going on and some disturbing trends. The preface said: "with the downward direction of our country and increasing world tension, a strong inner urge told the author to get his thoughts documented". The downward direction is not only a strong and difficult comment to make, but also a foreign idea to historic U. S., which has been a superpower, both economically and militarily, for over a century. The reader may ask then, please define downward direction. The following are some examples:

1. The U. S. debt has risen from five trillion dollars in 2008, a record at that time, to eighteen trillion by the end of 2014. GDP is seventeen trillion in 2014.
2. For the first time in U. S. history the credit rating was downgraded
3. China carries most of our debt
4. The U. S. has a record number of people on food stamps
5. Government calculations for inflation and unemployment have changed from historic formulas to show smaller numbers, thus lowering the Misery Index, perhaps by half or more. The Misery Index is inflation plus unemployment.
6. Minority unemployment has soared, especially for the youth
7. Take home pay for workers has decreased
8. The federal government has been printing money
9. Much of our freedom has been lost over time. The Environmental Protection Agency has grown to an army of unelected bureaucrats who are micromanaging our lives down to light bulbs and toilets

10. Approval ratings for the current president is around forty percent, congress is much lower
11. The space program has been gutted
12. Our boundaries are insecure. Millions of illegal are here and continue to come unchecked for disease or terrorist possibilities
13. The disintegration of the family and growth of single mothers and gay marriage
14. Veteran's hospitals, chartered to care for veterans, are a disaster with long waiting lines and falsification of records
15. Planning to downsize the military at a time of increasing world tensions

Perhaps the epitome of the decline is the city of Detroit. That once proud city of over a million people, and the hub of the U. S. auto industry, is now bankrupt with a population one fourth the peak. Its infrastructure in many places resembles a third world country. Many other cities are either bankrupt or are close. How does something like that happen? Obviously the politicians had a major contributing role. The unions demanding exorbitant wages and benefits had a role also.

The unheeded lesson here is not to spend more than your income. The Constitution of most states require a balanced budget. Families and individuals are also governed by a balanced budget. No amendment for a balanced budget is in the Constitution, yet. Only the federal government can print money. So, the author would like to ask the reader the same question Ronald Reagan asked Jimmy Carter in their presidential debate in 1980. Are you better off now than you were four years ago? Or today, are you better off than you were six years ago?

Two other arenas are on the heels of Detroit, the manufacturing and energy sectors of our economy. As you know, the manufacturing sector has almost lost industries such as clothing and steel. High taxes and environmental regulations have driven these and other industries overseas. The auto industry was reeling also, but got an education about quality from foreign manufacturers.

The energy sector, primarily oil and coal, are the victims of over regulations, which is driven by the environmental lobby, who our president is beholden to. God put those minerals on earth. Both should be and can be used responsibly as good stewards. The irony is that even if oil and coal could be purified as drinking water, it would be an exercise in futility unless the rest of the world follows suit.

U. S. is almost beholden to Islamic nations for oil and they don't like us. Also the environmentalists, via our president, have stopped the Keystone Pipeline, which could bring oil to U. S. refineries. The pipeline could also create much needed jobs. States such as Ohio, Pennsylvania, West Virginia and others have enough coal to last hundreds of years. The gasoline our cars use is mandated to contain ethanol, a corn byproduct for cleaner exhaust. Ethanol has significantly less energy than regular unleaded gasoline. As a result, more has to be burned for the same power output. Also, a significant part of corn production goes to ethanol production. How does that balance with using the corn to feed starving people? There are unintended consequences!

For a superpower to experience a downward direction, something changed. Either some event or events would have to have happened or a series of small individual changes happened to creep in over time to reach some tipping point. There are three words that the author believes that can account for the downward direction of any country. They are: apathy, encroachment and inflation. Let's take them one at a time.

Apathy

The definition of apathy is: lack of interest; lack of emotion; listless condition; not interested, not caring. In the author's words; not interested, not caring. One of the precious rights in a democracy is to vote. In the U. S., the percentile of eligible voters that actually vote is in the thirty percentile. Many people in other countries only dream of voting. Over time, that makes it a lot easier for a rogue group to enact laws, like a group that believes the Constitution is a living document, to be interpreted as needed.

Encroachment

The definition of encroachment is: to advance beyond the normal, original or customary limits or to make inroads. In the authors words: the gradual loss of freedom, gradual growth of government. When the U. S. became a self governing country, the federal government was very small. Over the years, with good intentions and the liberal use of the word fair, the federal government has grown to virtually an uncontrollable size. Of course the U. S. is a different country now then when it was founded. Some change was in order. When, however, the constitution is treated as a living document, the interpretation can be by whoever is in power. If that is the case, you have a dictatorship. The framers were concerned about the size of the federal government. Are we now at that tipping point? If not, we are getting close.

Inflation

The definition of inflation is a little more complicated. Its definition is: an increase in the money in circulation resulting in a sudden fall in its value and rise in prices; it may be caused by an increase in the volume of paper money issued or gold mined; or a relative increase in expenditures as when the supply of goods fails to meet the demand. Whew! In the author's words: government running up the national debt and printing paper money to pay for it. Interest rates today are being held artificially low. When THEY WILL RISE, inflation will raise its ugly head. For examples, the reader can study Germany in the 1920's and Argentina in the 1980's.

Here are some examples of inflation in U. S. over time:

Goods	1940 Cost	2014 Cost
Quart of milk	$ 0.14	$ 1.80
Loaf of bread	$ 0.18	$ 2.00 – 4.00
Pound of butter	$ 0.50	$ 4.00 – 5.00
Pound of ground beef	$ 0.30	$5.00 +
Gallon of gasoline	$ 0.25	$ 3.50 – 4.50
An automobile	$ 1,000.00 +/-	$ 20.000.00 +/-
Single family house	$ 5,000.00 +/-	$ 100,000.00 +/-

The author remembers the 1940 costs as he used to go to the local grocery store for his parents. Today, and for many years, the U. S. dollar has been the currency most other countries' currency is pegged to for commerce between the countries. Gold used to be the benchmark. With continuous deficit spending and printing money, the U. S. currency is decreasing in value. If this continues unabated, a different currency or standard will be the new basis of exchange between countries. Already there is talk of such an effort. If the U. S. dollar is no longer the basis of exchange, welcome to hyper inflation. This could be the U. S. Achilles Heel!

Our President

The author has tried to minimize politics, but that is imbedded in the U. S. downward direction. It is his belief, that as a good citizen, the laws enacted by our governments should be obeyed. That is why we have the best self governing system ever devised by man. Leaders, like all of us, are not perfect and sin. When we see lies and injustice, it is our constitutional right to voice objections, suggest change and work through our political system. That is why the Declaration of Independence and the Constitution of the United States are included.

When Barak Obama was elected president, the country was elated to have finally gotten past their race stigma and elected a black president. He came out of nowhere with a scant resume, but with extraordinary rhetorical skills. He promised to fundamentally change the U. S., although the meaning of fundamentally change was illusive. He also promised that his administration would be the most transparent ever. Most of the press was enamored with him, with little vetting. Isn't that why the Constitution guarantees a free press? There was some speculation that fundamentally change meant a huge transfer of wealth from the haves to the have-nots, in the name of fairness (income redistribution).

At the time of his election, his party captured both houses of congress, yielding a one party rule. His signature piece of legislation was the Affordable Care Act (ACA), a radical transformation of the greatest health care system in the world to a government run system, a frontrunner to socialized medicine. The stated reason was so some thirty to forty million uninsured could be insured. It was only fair that everybody had insurance. If one ponders the word fair, they would conclude it is like the word beauty, only meaningful to the beholder.

Some facts about the ACA. President Obama promised that you could keep your present insurance and doctor, period, at least thirty times on television. He also promised that the ACA would save an average family $ 2,500.00 a year. Ironically, the Speaker of the

House said "we have to pass it to find out what is in it". As we know, what the president said wasn't factual. The dictionary defines a lie as: to utter fabrication with an intent to deceive; to utter falsehoods habitually; to cause an incorrect impression; to present misleading appearance and to deceive one. In the author's words, a lie is a lie, period. Yes, the promises were lies. If this was a previous era in U. S., people would say snake oil salesman.

As we all know, the ACA was mostly crafted behind closed doors, with no amendments possible and with voting approval by one party. As we also know, some long standing Congressional rules were changed to get the vote. The other irony now is that when the ACA is fully implemented, there will still be twenty to thirty million without health insurance. Does this sound like a banana republic?

In addition, the implementation, by law, was October 1, 2013 with enrollees having until January 1, 2014 to enroll without penalty. The rollout was a disaster. The web sites for enrolling and for paying the policy premiums were not complete. To date they have not been completed and certified. Many people still do not know whether they are insured.

President Obama, with executive orders, has given waivers to Congress, unions and others. He has also issued executive orders delaying parts of the ACA. Both sets of orders are legislative functions per the Constitution. Law suits are in process to stop the executive orders. Surveys show the majority of citizens do not want the ACA. In August 2014, the president has threatened to give amnesty to millions of people, here illegally, through executive orders because Congress has not acted. If so, what will be the next laws scrapped?

In addition, investigations into the ACA and other controversial activities are being stonewalled as:

1. Operation Fast Track – guns from U. S. used by Mexicans to kill a border agent
2. Benghazi, Libya – the killing of the U. S. ambassador, two Navy Seals and a guard
3. Not processing tax exempt applications for opposing party legal political activities
4. Not enforcing the U. S. border security, enhancing the risk of terrorists and disease coming in U. S.
5. Spying on reporters
6. The VA hospital scandal – falsifying records and long service delays

So much for transparency.

Perhaps some readers remember an interesting insight into the president's thought process that he said during a reelection rally. "Remember, you didn't build it, the government built it". The framers might take exception with that statement. Two other insights are worthy of noting. The president has always blamed someone else for what has happened on his watch, particularly the former president, George W. Bush. In addition, he is almost always surprised when something controversy happens on his watch. He says he finds out from the news media. A respected leader takes ownership of problems and solves them. On the other hand, it is easier to surprise a rookie. Prior to his first election, there was little vetting by the press as to what his charter was as a community organizer. For all we know, the operation of a lemonade stand is a step above.

The President of the United States is sworn in in January after each four year election cycle. The ceremony has the new president, with his hand on the Bible, repeat the words used since George Washington did his: "I do solemnly swear (or affirm) that I will faithfully execute the Office of President of the United States and will to the best of my ability, preserve, protect and defend the Constitution of the United States". Words have meaning. Perhaps the scariest sign of a nation in decline is the leader selectively enforcing the law. That leads to no law other than the leader's, then eventually to a dictatorship. Two glaring examples of many are the border security and the Defense of Marriage Act. A country without a border is not a country.

In the book, "The Decline of the Roman Empire", the author Edward Gibbon (1737-1794), after his analysis, lists eleven characteristics of their decay. From an internet download, they are:

1. No fault divorce
2. Increase disrespect of parenthood and parents
3. Meaningless marriage rites and ceremonies
4. Defamation of national hero's
5. Acceptance of alternate marriage forms
6. Widespread attitudes of feminism, narcissism and hedonism
7. Propagation of anti family sentiment
8. Acceptance of most forms of adultery
9. Rebellious children
10. Increased juvenile delinquency
11. Common acceptance of all forms of sexual perversions

The reader can score the U. S. report card.

The book, "Rules for Radicals" by Saul Alinsky may also give a clue as to what is going on. Here are some rules from that book, downloaded from the internet:

1. Politics is all about power relations, but to advance one's power, one must couch one's position in the language of morality. (fairness)

2. There are three kinds of people in world: rich and powerful oppressors; the poor and disenchanted and the middle class whose apathy perpetuates the status quo

3. Change is brought about through relentless agitation and trouble making of a kind that radically disrupts society as it is.

4. There can be no conversation between the organizer and his opponents. The later must be depicted as evil.

5. The organizer can never focus on a single issue. He must move inexhaustibly from one issue to the next.

6. Taunt one's opponent to the point that they label you a dangerous enemy of the establishment.

That is some game plan! Let us pray it is not the president's. If it is, he is well on the way to destroying the U.S.

Power can be intoxicating. Power is like fire. It can be used for good things or for bad things. Power can be used for creature comforts or to enslave. Fire can be used for creature comforts and to destroy. A truism the author heard about years ago was: "if you ignore reality, it will automatically work against you".

By now, some readers may have the opinion that the author is a racist. Can someone criticize the president's policies without being called a racist? This is still the United States of America. The author's firm belief is that all people are children of God, but there is evil in the world. Look no further than the Islamic terrorists.

The author also subscribes to the comments of Vince Lombardi, legendary coach of the Green Bay Packers. According to Jerry Kramer's book, "Instant Replay", one day a group of civil rights people came into the Packer office and told Coach Lombardi they were there to interview the Packer's black athletes. He told them they couldn't because there weren't any black athletes, only athletes.

Yes, there are racists in the U. S. There are also race baiters, who play the race card in an honest debate because they have little else to offer. So, who is worse, a racist or a race baiter? The answer is that both are despicable and have no standing in any debate. They need to repent and ask God's forgiveness.

While the role of America is not mentioned in the Bible, obviously it still plays a role today. A case could be made for parts of Dr. Jeremiah's possible explanations. The declines could also be reversed. It would be a herculean task with a new political will to stop the declines and reverse course. If enough people care, it could happen, but not overnight.

2014 Election Update

Now that the mid-term elections are over, the U. S. voters have spoken their desires for their political representation. The Republican party has swept the elections on all levels, gaining control of Congress and significantly increasing gains in state elections. The new congressional leaders seem to understand the message from the people for a new U. S. direction.

The President has given mixed messages. While speaking in amiable tones of working together, he has strongly restated his intent to go around Congress and use executive orders, by year end, and give some sort of legal standing to millions of people, here illegally, not willing to wait for Congress to act. Surveys show that over seventy percent of the people do not want that action taken by the President. Per the Constitution, Congress has the power to enact laws. Without securing the border first, the floodgates for more illegal will remain open. What is so difficult about understanding the meaning of the word illegal?

The voting statements by the people show that they care about the downward direction of U. S. That is a good start to reverse course. Without the politicians on board, however, the probability of reversing course is at a standstill. It would be well to heed the people's wishes. Talk is cheap. Actions speak much louder.

Here is an interesting what if scenario to ponder about the possible timing of the end time. What country, other than U. S., would have both the capabilities and desire to stand up to the despots bent on destroying Israel? It is the author's prayer that the President and Congress can work together to reverse the downward direction. Time will tell.

Rapture

Many end time Biblical Prophesy scholars are in agreement that the next major end time event will be the Rapture. The reestablishment of the state of Israel was the major event to cause the Rapture clock to start ticking. The word rapture is not in the Bible. It is, however, a good way to describe the event. Paul describes the event in his first letter to the Thessalonians.

1 Thessalonians 4: 13-18

Now brothers, we do not want you to be ignorant about those who fall asleep, or grieve like the rest of the men, who have no hope. We believe that Jesus died and rose again and so we believe God will bring with Jesus those who have fallen asleep in him. According to his own word, we tell you who are still alive, who are left until the coming of the Lord will certainly not precede those who have fallen asleep. For the Lord himself will come down from heaven, with a loud command, with the voice of the archangel and with the trumpet call of God, and the dead in Christ will rise first. After that, we who are still alive and are left will be caught up together with them in the clouds to meet the Lord in the air. And so we will be with the Lord forever. Therefore, encourage each other with these words.

Paul also wrote to the Corinthians about the event.

1 Corinthians 15: 15-16

I will tell you a mystery. We will not all sleep but will be changed, in a flash, in a twinkling of an eye at the last trumpet. For the trumpet will sound, the dead will be raised imperishable and will be changed.

From the apostle John:

John 14: 2-4

In my Father's house, there are many rooms; if it were not so, I would have told you. And I am going there to prepare a place for you. And if I go and prepare a place for you, I will come back and take you to be with me that you also may be where I am.

As a result of the Rapture, Christians will be with the Lord forever. The whole world will be in an unimaginable turmoil then.

Revelation

The last book in the New Testament and Bible is Revelation. It is the revelation of Jesus Christ. The definition of revelation is: an act of making known or the thing made known. It deals with the return of Jesus Christ to earth to cleanse and setup His everlasting kingdom. Revelation is in three parts:

1. Things that were

2. Things that are
3. Things that are to be.

One of the Gospel writers, John, received the words while a prisoner on Patmos Island at the age of ninety. He was a prisoner because the Romans, at that time, were beginning to enforce emperor worship. The book of Revelation is rarely discussed. The author never remembers it as the basis of a sermon or discussed at a Bible study. That seems a little strange because a powerful verse is at the beginning.

Revelation 1:3

Blessed is the one that reads this prophesy, and blessed are those who hear it and take heart what is written in it, because the time is near.

In captivity, John heard a voice and described the person who he saw. Then Christ identified himself and told John to write down what he had seen, what is now and what will take place later. John was then instructed what to tell the angel of each of the seven churches that were: Ephesus, Smyrna, Pergamum, Thyatira, Sardis, Philadelphia and Laodicea. It was sort of a report card.

John then appeared to be at a door standing open in heaven. A voice said:

Revelation 4: 1-2

After this, I looked and there before me was a door standing open in heaven. And the voice I had first heard speaking to me like a trumpet said: "Come up here and I will show you what must take place after this". At once I was in the spirit and there before me was a throne in heaven with someone sitting on it.

Revelation 5: 1

Then I saw in the right hand of him who sat on the throne, a scroll with writing on both sides and sealed with seven seals.

The seals were then opened. The first seal showed a rider on a white horse and rode as conqueror. The second seal showed a rider on a red horse who was given the power to take peace from the earth and make men slay each other. The third seal showed a rider on a black horse holding a pair of scales saying a quart of wheat for a days wages. The fourth seal showed a rider on a pale horse. The rider was named Death and Hades, who were given the power over a fourth of the earth to kill by sword, famine, plague and wild beasts. The fifth showed the souls of those who had been slain because of the word of God. The sixth seal was opened and there was a greatearthquake. The seventh seal was opened and there was silence in heaven.

Then came the seven trumpets. The seven trumpets represent the final folly of Satan. The anti-Christ rules the world. He demands the honor of Christ. People can only buy or sell with his mark. In the trumpets, Satan is releasing his power to accomplish his objectives. The seven golden bowls are then released. They are God's answer to Satan's cunning work. The first bowl is ugly and painful sores. In the second bowl, the sea turns to blood. In the third bowl, rivers and springs of water turn to blood. From the fourth bowl, the sun scorches people with fire. Darkness comes with the fifth bowl.

Revelation 16: 12

The sixth angel poured out his bowl on the great river Euphrates and its water dried up to prepare the way for the kings of the East.

Revelation 16:16

Then they gathered the kings together to that place in Hebrew is called Armageddon.

The seventh angel poured out his bowl and a huge earthquake, the earth has never seen, occurred.

The Finale

Never in history have so many key players gained capabilities and new trends started at the same time, both gaining strength and incurring weakness. These conditions raise the probability of the final confrontations as stated in the Bible. Let's examine each of the key players and see what is going on now.

Israel

The Israelites, God's chosen people, became a nation again in 1948. Israel is surrounded by Islamic nations bent on her destruction. The Islamic nations have a population and territory advantage of at least thirty to one. Israel, however, is armed to the teeth and has won two major conflicts in the last fifty years. In recent times, the Islamic terrorists have resorted to almost constant guerilla tactics against Israel.

Iran

Today, Iran is a rich nation due to their oil reserves. They have missile capability to reach Israel and beyond now. In addition, they are closing in on becoming a nuclear nation. They are also funding other Islamic groups, who use guerilla tactics against Israel. They are allied with other Islamic nations and Russia against Israel.

Russia

Today Russia is reconstituting into a superpower. Their president has ideas of annexing, again, nations in the area that Russia annexed after World War Two, but are independent nations today. The first step was to invade Ukraine and annex the Crimean area. Former Russian citizens in Ukraine are rioting and have succeeded in downing a commercial aircraft killing three hundred passengers and crew. Russia is in the process of rebuilding her military. She has had nuclear capability since 1950 and missiles to reach anywhere. They are allies with Iran. In prophesy, they and Iran are the countries from the North.

United States

The lone superpower, militarily and economically, U. S. has been a strong supporter of Israel since it has become a nation in 1948. Recently, under a new U. S. president, relations with Israel have cooled. The U. S. president has openly criticized Israel while praising the Islamics. In addition, the U. S. is in a strong downward economic trend. At the same time, the president is disengaging from foreign involvement. Concurrently, the U. S. is under seize with people from Mexico and Latin America crossing our border at will. The president refuses to secure the border. This and other domestic issues are keeping U. S. more in focus on the home front. In addition, the president is planning to downsize the military to below pre World War Two levels. These events have emboldened the terrorists, Iran, Russia and others. It has shown weakness in U. S.

China

China today is well on its way to become a superpower, both militarily and economically. Their economy has grown very rapidly and is expected to pass U. S. in a few years. Today they hold most of the U. S. debt, another sign of U. S. weakness. Militarily they are growing and beginning to intimidate nearby territories. With a population of over a billion people, they are capable of fielding a huge army. Being a communist nation, they have commonalities with Russia. In prophesy they are the country of the East.

Africa

Africa has shed its past colonization and today is comprised mostly of independent nations. Much of Africa is strong Islamic, with some nations radical and some peaceful. While their military capabilities are localized, in concert they could constitute a significant force. In prophesy, they are the country of the South.

End Events

Once the Rapture occurs, all Christian people from U. S. and other Christians will be gone. With extreme upheaval in the world, some semblance of order will be sought. Enter a one world government, as predicted in the Bible. It should be relatively easy as the United Nations and the European Union already exist.

Prophesy says that a group of ten leaders will represent all the world areas at some point. Soon a charismatic leader will enter the scene. He will charm the ten area leaders and promise a plan to secure world peace. The plan is agreed to by all, including Israel and the Islamic nations. Tensions are eased. Israel is at peace with her Islamic neighbors. Then three of the leaders rebel against the world leader, who puts the revolt down. Meanwhile, Satan is ejected from heaven to earth.

Then Russia and Iran, who will be stirred up by Satan, will invade Israel, who is at peace with her neighbors. Their object is to destroy Israel, the Jews and plunder their wealth. God will intervene and rout the attackers with his weapons: a massive earthquake; creating confusion among the attackers; infect the attackers with disease and bring calamities from the sky – hailstones, fire and brimstones. The rout will be a massive feast for predators and vultures. Satan will thus be defeated in this attempt to destroy Israel.

Satan then regroups his forces. At some point, the world leader (anti Christ), will be mortally wounded, miraculously recover, proclaim he is Christ and demand to be worshiped. He then will impose extreme measures on the people. The people will only be able to buy and sell if they have his mark, 666, on their foreheads. All who refuse the mark will be killed. Anyone accepting the mark will receive the same fate as the anti Christ.

Gradually the whole world will rebel against the anti Christ because of not fulfilling his promises. Meanwhile, Satan has been hardening hearts. Then the armies of the kings of the South will attack the anti Christ, who has made his headquarters in a rebuilt Babylon. The remnants of the kings of theNorth will join the attack. The anti Christ will subdue these attacks. When the Euphrates dries up, it makes way for the kings of the East with an army of two hundred million.

Revelation 16:16

Then they gathered the kings together in the place that in Hebrew is called Armageddon.

Jesus Christ then comes down from heaven with his armies.

Revelation 19: 19-21

Then I saw the beast and the kings of the earth and their armies gathered together to make war against the rider on the horse and his army. But the beast was captured and with him the false prophet, who performed the miraculous signs on his behalf. With these signs he had deluded those who had received the mark of the beast and worshiped the image. The two of them were thrown alive into the fiery lake of burning sulfur. The rest of them were killed by the sword that came out of the mouth of the rider on the horse and all the birds gorged themselves on the flesh.

The Lord's kingdom on earth was then setup. For those who keep score, Jesus won, Satan lost

Chapter 5

What Can We Do?

1. First and foremost, get right with the Lord. Understand that the Bible is the word of God as He wanted us to know the truth. Accept the gift from Jesus Christ that He died on the cross for the payment of all of our sins and in believing in Him you will have eternal life.
2. Follow the great commandments of Jesus – love the Lord your God, love your neighbor as yourself and tell the story of Jesus, especially to your family and friends.
3. Act as the prophet Micah wrote – do justice, love kindness and walk humbly before the Lord.
4. Be informed of worldly events, especially the U. S. events. Use multiple sources to get all sides of a story. Discuss events with family and friends.
5. Understand the positions of political candidates on issues. VOTE!
6. Do not worry. Worry is a sign of distrust of the Lord.
7. Go about your normal life. For Christians, the Rapture could come at any time or years from now. Only God knows. Trust Him. He is a loving God.

Now, naysayers may ridicule some of the above. The author would like to ask them three questions.

1. What is the harm and who is harmed?
2. What is the reward if the Rapture happens in our lifetime?
3. What is the peril to those left behind if the Rapture happens in our lifetime?

Thank you for reading the book. May God bless you, your family and the U. S.

Appendix A

The Declaration of Independence of the United States

July 4, 1776

The Declaration of Independence: A Transcription

IN CONGRESS, July 4, 1776.

The unanimous Declaration of the thirteen united States of America,

When in the Course of human events, it becomes necessary for one people to dissolve the political bands which have connected them with another, and to assume among the powers of the earth, the separate and equal station to which the Laws of Nature and of Nature's God entitle them, a decent respect to the opinions of mankind requires that they should declare the causes which impel them to the separation.

We hold these truths to be self-evident, that all men are created equal, that they are endowed by their Creator with certain unalienable Rights, that among these are Life, Liberty and the pursuit of Happiness.--That to secure these rights, Governments are instituted among Men, deriving their just powers from the consent of the governed, --That whenever any Form of Government becomes destructive of these ends, it is the Right of the People to alter or to abolish it, and to institute new Government, laying its foundation on such principles and organizing its powers in such form, as to them shall seem most likely to effect their Safety and Happiness. Prudence, indeed, will dictate that Governments long established should not be changed for light and transient causes; and accordingly all experience hath shewn, that mankind are more disposed to suffer, while evils are sufferable, than to right themselves by abolishing the forms to which they are accustomed. But when a long train of abuses and usurpations, pursuing invariably the same Object evinces a design to reduce them under absolute Despotism, it is their right, it is their duty, to throw off such Government, and to provide new Guards for their future security.--Such has been the patient sufferance of these Colonies; and such is now the necessity which constrains them to alter their former Systems of Government. The history of the present King of Great Britain is a history of repeated injuries and usurpations, all having in direct object the establishment of an absolute Tyranny over these States. To prove this, let Facts be submitted to a candid world.

He has refused his Assent to Laws, the most wholesome and necessary for the public good

He has forbidden his Governors to pass Laws of immediate and pressing importance, unless suspended in their operation till his Assent should be obtained; and when so suspended, he has utterly neglected to attend to them.

He has refused to pass other Laws for the accommodation of large districts of people, unless those people would relinquish the right of Representation in the Legislature, a right inestimable to them and formidable to tyrants only.

He has called together legislative bodies at places unusual, uncomfortable, and distant from the depository of their public Records, for the sole purpose of fatiguing them into compliance with his measures.

He has dissolved Representative Houses repeatedly, for opposing with manly firmness his invasions on the rights of the people.

He has refused for a long time, after such dissolutions, to cause others to be elected; whereby the Legislative powers, incapable of Annihilation, have returned to the People at large for their exercise; the State remaining in the mean time exposed to all the dangers of invasion from without, and convulsions within.

He has endeavoured to prevent the population of these States; for that purpose obstructing the Laws for Naturalization of Foreigners; refusing to pass others to encourage their migrations hither, and raising the conditions of new Appropriations of Lands.

He has obstructed the Administration of Justice, by refusing his Assent to Laws for establishing Judiciary powers.

He has made Judges dependent on his Will alone, for the tenure of their offices, and the amount and payment of their salaries.

He has erected a multitude of New Offices, and sent hither swarms of Officers to harrass our people, and eat out their substance.

He has kept among us, in times of peace, Standing Armies without the Consent of our legislatures.

He has affected to render the Military independent of and superior to the Civil power.

He has combined with others to subject us to a jurisdiction foreign to our constitution, and unacknowledged by our laws; giving his Assent to their Acts of pretended Legislation:

For Quartering large bodies of armed troops among us:

For protecting them, by a mock Trial, from punishment for any Murders which they should commit on the Inhabitants of these States:

For cutting off our Trade with all parts of the world:

For imposing Taxes on us without our Consent:

For depriving us in many cases, of the benefits of Trial by Jury:

For transporting us beyond Seas to be tried for pretended offences

For abolishing the free System of English Laws in a neighbouring Province, establishing therein an Arbitrary government, and enlarging its Boundaries so as to render it at once an example and fit instrument for introducing the same absolute rule into these Colonies:

For taking away our Charters, abolishing our most valuable Laws, and altering fundamentally the Forms of our Governments:

For suspending our own Legislatures, and declaring themselves invested with power to legislate for us in all cases whatsoever.

He has abdicated Government here, by declaring us out of his Protection and waging War against us.

He has plundered our seas, ravaged our Coasts, burnt our towns, and destroyed the lives of our people.

He is at this time transporting large Armies of foreign Mercenaries to compleat the works of death, desolation and tyranny, already begun with circumstances of Cruelty & perfidy scarcely paralleled in the most barbarous ages, and totally unworthy the Head of a civilized nation.

He has constrained our fellow Citizens taken Captive on the high Seas to bear Arms against their Country, to become the executioners of their friends and Brethren, or to fall themselves by their Hands.

He has excited domestic insurrections amongst us, and has endeavoured to bring on the inhabitants of our frontiers, the merciless Indian Savages, whose known rule of warfare, is an undistinguished destruction of all ages, sexes and conditions.

In every stage of these Oppressions We have Petitioned for Redress in the most humble terms: Our repeated Petitions have been answered only by repeated injury. A Prince whose character is thus marked by every act which may define a Tyrant, is unfit to be the ruler of a free people.

Nor have We been wanting in attentions to our Brittish brethren. We have warned them from time to time of attempts by their legislature to extend an unwarrantable jurisdiction over us. We have reminded them of the circumstances of our emigration and settlement here.

We have appealed to their native justice and magnanimity, and we have conjured them by the ties of our common kindred to disavow these usurpations, which, would inevitably interrupt our connections and correspondence. They too have been deaf to the voice of justice and of consanguinity. We must, therefore, acquiesce in the necessity, which denounces our Separation, and hold them, as we hold the rest of mankind, Enemies in War, in Peace Friends.

We, therefore, the Representatives of the united States of America, in General Congress, Assembled, appealing to the Supreme Judge of the world for the rectitude of our intentions, do, in the Name, and by Authority of the good People of these Colonies, solemnly publish and declare, That these United Colonies are, and of Right ought to be Free and Independent States; that they are Absolved from all Allegiance to the British Crown, and that all political connection between them and the State of Great Britain, is and ought to be totally dissolved; and that as Free and Independent States, they have full Power to levy War, conclude Peace, contract Alliances, establish Commerce, and to do all other Acts and Things which Independent States may of right do. And for the support of this Declaration, with a firm reliance on the protection of divine Providence, we mutually pledge to each other our Lives, our Fortunes and our sacred Honor.

The 56 signatures on the Declaration appear in the positions indicated:

Column 1
Georgia:

> Button Gwinnett
> Lyman Hall
> George Walton

Column 2
North Carolina:

William Hooper
Joseph Hewes
John Penn

South Carolina:

Edward Rutledge
Thomas Heyward, Jr.
Thomas Lynch, Jr.
Arthur Middleton

Column 3
Massachusetts:

John Hancock

Maryland:

Samuel Chase
William Paca
Thomas Stone
Charles Carroll of Carrollton

Virginia:

George Wythe
Richard Henry Lee
Thomas Jefferson
Benjamin Harrison
Thomas Nelson, Jr.
Francis Lightfoot Lee
Carter Braxton

Column 4
Pennsylvania:

Robert Morris
Benjamin Rush
Benjamin Franklin
John Morton
George Clymer
James Smith
George Taylor
James Wilson
George Ross

Delaware:

Caesar Rodney
George Read
Thomas McKean

Column 5
New York:

William Floyd
Philip Livingston
Francis Lewis
Lewis Morris

New Jersey:

Richard Stockton
John Witherspoon
Francis Hopkinson
John Hart
Abraham Clark

Column 6
New Hampshire:

Josiah Bartlett
William Whipple

Massachusetts:

Samuel Adams
John Adams
Robert Treat Paine
Elbridge Gerry

Rhode Island:

Stephen Hopkins
William Ellery

Connecticut:

Roger Sherman
Samuel Huntington
William Williams
Oliver Wolcott

New Hampshire:

Matthew Thornton

Appendix B

The Constitution of the United States

The Constitution of the United States: A Transcription

Note: The following text is a transcription of the Constitution as it was inscribed by Jacob Shallus on parchment (the document on display in the Rotunda at the National Archives Museum.) Items that are hyperlinked have since been amended or superseded. The authenticated text of the Constitution can be found on the website of the Government Printing Office.

We the People of the United States, in Order to form a more perfect Union, establish Justice, insure domestic Tranquility, provide for the common defence, promote the general Welfare, and secure the Blessings of Liberty to ourselves and our Posterity, do ordain and establish this Constitution for the United States of America.

Article. I.

Section. 1.

All legislative Powers herein granted shall be vested in a Congress of the United States, which shall consist of a Senate and House of Representatives.

Section. 2.

The House of Representatives shall be composed of Members chosen every second Year by the People of the several States, and the Electors in each State shall have the Qualifications requisite for Electors of the most numerous Branch of the State Legislature.

No Person shall be a Representative who shall not have attained to the Age of twenty five Years, and been seven Years a Citizen of the United States, and who shall not, when elected, be an Inhabitant of that State in which he shall be chosen.

Representatives and direct Taxes shall be apportioned among the several States which may be included within this Union, according to their respective Numbers, which shall be determined by adding to the whole Number of free Persons, including those bound to Service for a Term of Years, and excluding Indians not taxed, three fifths of all other Persons. The actual Enumeration shall be made within three Years after the first Meeting of the Congress of the United States, and within every subsequent Term of ten Years, in such Manner as they shall by Law direct. The Number of Representatives shall not exceed one for every thirty Thousand, but each State shall have at Least one Representative; and until such enumeration shall be made, the State of New Hampshire shall be entitled to chuse three, Massachusetts eight, Rhode-Island and Providence Plantations one, Connecticut five, New-York six, New Jersey four, Pennsylvania eight, Delaware one, Maryland six, Virginia ten, North Carolina five, South Carolina five, and Georgia three.

When vacancies happen in the Representation from any State, the Executive Authority thereof shall issue Writs of Election to fill such Vacancies.

The House of Representatives shall chuse their Speaker and other Officers; and shall have the sole Power of Impeachment.

Section. 3.

The Senate of the United States shall be composed of two Senators from each State, <u>chosen by the Legislature</u> thereof, for six Years; and each Senator shall have one Vote.

Immediately after they shall be assembled in Consequence of the first Election, they shall be divided as equally as may be into three Classes. The Seats of the Senators of the first Class shall be vacated at the Expiration of the second Year, of the second Class at the Expiration of the fourth Year, and of the third Class at the Expiration of the sixth Year, so that one third may be chosen every second Year; <u>and if Vacancies happen by Resignation, or otherwise, during the Recess of the Legislature of any State, the Executive thereof may make temporary Appointments until the next Meeting of the Legislature, which shall then fill such Vacancies.</u>

No Person shall be a Senator who shall not have attained to the Age of thirty Years, and been nine Years a Citizen of the United States, and who shall not, when elected, be an Inhabitant of that State for which he shall be chosen.

The Vice President of the United States shall be President of the Senate, but shall have no Vote, unless they be equally divided.

The Senate shall chuse their other Officers, and also a President pro tempore, in the Absence of the Vice President, or when he shall exercise the Office of President of the United States.

The Senate shall have the sole Power to try all Impeachments. When sitting for that Purpose, they shall be on Oath or Affirmation. When the President of the United States is tried, the Chief Justice shall preside: And no Person shall be convicted without the Concurrence of two thirds of the Members present.

Judgment in Cases of Impeachment shall not extend further than to removal from Office, and disqualification to hold and enjoy any Office of honor, Trust or Profit under the United States: but the Party convicted shall nevertheless be liable and subject to Indictment, Trial, Judgment and Punishment, according to Law.

Section. 4.

The Times, Places and Manner of holding Elections for Senators and Representatives, shall be prescribed in each State by the Legislature thereof; but the Congress may at any time by Law make or alter such Regulations, except as to the Places of chusing Senators.

The Congress shall assemble at least once in every Year, and such Meeting shall <u>be on the first Monday in December</u>, unless they shall by Law appoint a different Day.

Section. 5.

Each House shall be the Judge of the Elections, Returns and Qualifications of its own Members, and a Majority of each shall constitute a Quorum to do Business; but a smaller Number may adjourn from day to day, and may be authorized to compel the Attendance of absent Members, in such Manner, and under such Penalties as each House may provide.

Each House may determine the Rules of its Proceedings, punish its Members for disorderly Behaviour, and, with the Concurrence of two thirds, expel a Member.

Each House shall keep a Journal of its Proceedings, and from time to time publish the same, excepting such Parts as may in their Judgment require Secrecy; and the Yeas and Nays of the Members of either House on any question shall, at the Desire of one fifth of those Present, be entered on the Journal.

Neither House, during the Session of Congress, shall, without the Consent of the other, adjourn for more than three days, nor to any other Place than that in which the two Houses shall be sitting.

Section. 6.

The Senators and Representatives shall receive a Compensation for their Services, to be ascertained by Law, and paid out of the Treasury of the United States. They shall in all Cases, except Treason, Felony and Breach of the Peace, be privileged from Arrest during their Attendance at the Session of their respective Houses, and in going to and returning from the same; and for any Speech or Debate in either House, they shall not be questioned in any other Place.

No Senator or Representative shall, during the Time for which he was elected, be appointed to any civil Office under the Authority of the United States, which shall have been created, or the Emoluments whereof shall have been encreased during such time; and no Person holding any Office under the United States, shall be a Member of either House during his Continuance in Office.

Section. 7.

All Bills for raising Revenue shall originate in the House of Representatives; but the Senate may propose or concur with Amendments as on other Bills.

Every Bill which shall have passed the House of Representatives and the Senate, shall, before it become a Law, be presented to the President of the United States; If he approve he shall sign it, but if not he shall return it, with his Objections to that House in which it shall have originated, who shall enter the Objections at large on their Journal, and proceed to reconsider it. If after such Reconsideration two thirds of that House shall agree to pass the Bill, it shall be sent, together with the Objections, to the other House, by which it shall likewise be reconsidered, and if approved by two thirds of that House, it shall become a Law. But in all such Cases the Votes of both Houses shall be determined by yeas and Nays, and the Names of the Persons voting for and against the Bill shall be entered on the Journal of each House respectively. If any Bill shall not be returned by the President within ten Days (Sundays excepted) after it shall have been presented to him, the Same shall be a Law, in like Manner as if he had signed it, unless the Congress by their Adjournment prevent its Return, in which Case it shall not be a Law.

Every Order, Resolution, or Vote to which the Concurrence of the Senate and House of Representatives may be necessary (except on a question of Adjournment) shall be presented to the President of the United States; and before the Same shall take Effect, shall be approved by him, or being disapproved by him, shall be repassed by two thirds of the Senate and House of Representatives, according to the Rules and Limitations prescribed in the Case of a Bill.

Section. 8.

The Congress shall have Power To lay and collect Taxes, Duties, Imposts and Excises, to pay the Debts and provide for the common Defence and general Welfare of the United States; but all Duties, Imposts and Excises shall be uniform throughout the United States;

To borrow Money on the credit of the United States;

To regulate Commerce with foreign Nations, and among the several States, and with the Indian Tribes;

To establish an uniform Rule of Naturalization, and uniform Laws on the subject of Bankruptcies throughout the United States;

To coin Money, regulate the Value thereof, and of foreign Coin, and fix the Standard of Weights and Measures;

To provide for the Punishment of counterfeiting the Securities and current Coin of the United States;

To establish Post Offices and post Roads;

To promote the Progress of Science and useful Arts, by securing for limited Times to Authors and Inventors the exclusive Right to their respective Writings and Discoveries;

To constitute Tribunals inferior to the supreme Court;

To define and punish Piracies and Felonies committed on the high Seas, and Offences against the Law of Nations;

To declare War, grant Letters of Marque and Reprisal, and make Rules concerning Captures on Land and Water;

To raise and support Armies, but no Appropriation of Money to that Use shall be for a longer Term than two Years;

To provide and maintain a Navy;

To make Rules for the Government and Regulation of the land and naval Forces;

To provide for calling forth the Militia to execute the Laws of the Union, suppress Insurrections and repel Invasions;

To provide for organizing, arming, and disciplining, the Militia, and for governing such Part of them as may be employed in the Service of the United States, reserving to the States respectively, the Appointment of the Officers, and the Authority of training the Militia according to the discipline prescribed by Congress;

To exercise exclusive Legislation in all Cases whatsoever, over such District (not exceeding ten Miles square) as may, by Cession of particular States, and the Acceptance of Congress, become the Seat of the Government of the United States, and to exercise like Authority over all Places purchased by the Consent of the Legislature of the State in which the Same shall be, for the Erection of Forts, Magazines, Arsenals, dock-Yards, and other needful Buildings;—And

To make all Laws which shall be necessary and proper for carrying into Execution the foregoing Powers, and all other Powers vested by this Constitution in the Government of the United States, or in any Department or Officer thereof.

Section. 9.

The Migration or Importation of such Persons as any of the States now existing shall think proper to admit, shall not be prohibited by the Congress prior to the Year one thousand eight hundred and eight, but a Tax or duty may be imposed on such Importation, not exceeding ten dollars for each Person.

The Privilege of the Writ of Habeas Corpus shall not be suspended, unless when in Cases of Rebellion or Invasion the public Safety may require it.

No Bill of Attainder or ex post facto Law shall be passed.

No Capitation, or other direct, Tax shall be laid, <u>unless in Proportion to the Census or enumeration herein before directed to be taken.</u>

No Tax or Duty shall be laid on Articles exported from any State.

No Preference shall be given by any Regulation of Commerce or Revenue to the Ports of one State over those of another: nor shall Vessels bound to, or from, one State, be obliged to enter, clear, or pay Duties in another.

No Money shall be drawn from the Treasury, but in Consequence of Appropriations made by Law; and a regular Statement and Account of the Receipts and Expenditures of all public Money shall be published from time to time.

No Title of Nobility shall be granted by the United States: And no Person holding any Office of Profit or Trust under them, shall, without the Consent of the Congress, accept of any present,

Emolument, Office, or Title, of any kind whatever, from any King, Prince, or foreign State.

Section. 10.

No State shall enter into any Treaty, Alliance, or Confederation; grant Letters of Marque and Reprisal; coin Money; emit Bills of Credit; make any Thing but gold and silver Coin a Tender in Payment of Debts; pass any Bill of Attainder, ex post facto Law, or Law impairing the Obligation of Contracts, or grant any Title of Nobility.

No State shall, without the Consent of the Congress, lay any Imposts or Duties on Imports or Exports, except what may be absolutely necessary for executing it's inspection Laws: and the net Produce of all Duties and Imposts, laid by any State on Imports or Exports, shall be for the Use of the Treasury of the United States; and all such Laws shall be subject to the Revision and Controul of the Congress.

No State shall, without the Consent of Congress, lay any Duty of Tonnage, keep Troops, or Ships of War in time of Peace, enter into any Agreement or Compact with another State, or with a foreign Power, or engage in War, unless actually invaded, or in such imminent Danger as will not admit of delay.

Article. II.

Section. 1.

The executive Power shall be vested in a President of the United States of America. He shall hold his Office during the Term of four

Years, and, together with the Vice President, chosen for the same Term, be elected, as follows

Each State shall appoint, in such Manner as the Legislature thereof may direct, a Number of Electors, equal to the whole Number of Senators and Representatives to which the State may be entitled in the Congress: but no Senator or Representative, or Person holding an Office of Trust or Profit under the United States, shall be appointed an Elector.

The Electors shall meet in their respective States, and vote by Ballot for two Persons, of whom one at least shall not be an Inhabitant of the same State with themselves. And they shall make a List of all the Persons voted for, and of the Number of Votes for each; which List they shall sign and certify, and transmit sealed to the Seat of the Government of the United States, directed to the President of the Senate. The President of the Senate shall, in the Presence of the Senate and House of Representatives, open all the Certificates, and the Votes shall then be counted. The Person having the greatest Number of Votes shall be the President, if such Number be a Majority of the whole Number of Electors appointed; and if there be more than one who have such Majority, and have an equal Number of Votes, then the House of Representatives shall immediately chuse by Ballot one of them for President; and if no Person have a Majority, then from the five highest on the List the said House shall in like Manner chuse the President. But in chusing the President, the Votes shall be taken by States, the Representation from each State having one Vote; A quorum for this Purpose shall consist of a Member or Members from two thirds of the States, and a Majority of all the States shall be necessary to a Choice. In every Case, after the Choice of the President, the Person having the greatest Number of Votes of the Electors shall be the Vice President. But if there should remain two or more who have equal Votes, the Senate shall chuse from them by Ballot the Vice President.

The Congress may determine the Time of chusing the Electors, and the Day on which they shall give their Votes; which Day shall be the same throughout the United States.

No Person except a natural born Citizen, or a Citizen of the United States, at the time of the Adoption of this Constitution, shall be eligible to the Office of President; neither shall any Person be eligible to that Office who shall not have attained to the Age of thirty five Years, and been fourteen Years a Resident within the United States.

<u>In Case of the Removal of the President from Office, or of his Death, Resignation, or Inability to discharge the Powers and Duties of the said Office, the Same shall devolve on the Vice President, and the Congress may by Law provide for the Case of Removal, Death, Resignation or Inability, both of the President and Vice President, declaring what Officer shall then act as President, and such Officer shall act accordingly, until the Disability be removed, or a President shall be elected</u>.

The President shall, at stated Times, receive for his Services, a Compensation, which shall neither be encreased nor diminished during the Period for which he shall have been elected, and he shall not receive within that Period any other Emolument from the United States, or any of them.

Before he enter on the Execution of his Office, he shall take the following Oath or Affirmation:—"I do solemnly swear (or affirm) that I will faithfully execute the Office of President of the United States, and will to the best of my Ability, preserve, protect and defend the Constitution of the United States."

Section. 2.

The President shall be Commander in Chief of the Army and Navy of the United States, and of the Militia of the several States, when called into the actual Service of the United States; he may require the Opinion, in writing, of the principal Officer in each of the executive Departments, upon any Subject relating to the Duties of their respective Offices, and he shall have Power to grant Reprieves and Pardons for Offences against the United States, except in Cases of Impeachment.

He shall have Power, by and with the Advice and Consent of the Senate, to make Treaties, provided two thirds of the Senators present concur; and he shall nominate, and by and with the Advice and Consent of the Senate, shall appoint Ambassadors, other public Ministers and Consuls, Judges of the supreme Court, and all other Officers of the United States, whose Appointments are not herein otherwise provided for, and which shall be established by Law: but the Congress may by Law vest the Appointment of such inferior Officers, as they think proper, in the President alone, in the Courts of Law, or in the Heads of Departments.

The President shall have Power to fill up all Vacancies that may happen during the Recess of the Senate, by granting Commissions which shall expire at the End of their next Session.

Section. 3.

He shall from time to time give to the Congress Information of the State of the Union, and recommend to their Consideration such Measures as he shall judge necessary and expedient; he may, on extraordinary Occasions, convene both Houses, or either of them, and in Case of Disagreement between them, with Respect to the Time of Adjournment, he may adjourn them to such Time as he shall think proper; he shall receive Ambassadors and other public Ministers; he shall take Care that the Laws be faithfully executed, and shall Commission all the Officers of the United States.

Section. 4.

The President, Vice President and all civil Officers of the United States, shall be removed from Office on Impeachment for, and Conviction of, Treason, Bribery, or other high Crimes and Misdemeanors.

Article III.

Section. 1.

The judicial Power of the United States, shall be vested in one supreme Court, and in such inferior Courts as the Congress may from time to time ordain and establish. The Judges, both of the supreme and inferior Courts, shall hold their Offices during good Behaviour, and shall, at stated Times, receive for their Services, a Compensation, which shall not be diminished during their Continuance in Office.

Section. 2.

The judicial Power shall extend to all Cases, in Law and Equity, arising under this Constitution, the Laws of the United States, and Treaties made, or which shall be made, under their Authority;—to all Cases affecting Ambassadors, other public Ministers and Consuls;—to all Cases of admiralty and maritime Jurisdiction;—to Controversies to which the United States shall be a Party;—to Controversies between two or more States;—between a State and Citizens of another State,—between Citizens of different States,—between Citizens of the same State claiming Lands under Grants of different States, and between a State, or the Citizens thereof, and foreign States, Citizens or Subjects.

In all Cases affecting Ambassadors, other public Ministers and Consuls, and those in which a State shall be Party, the supreme Court shall have original Jurisdiction. In all the other Cases before mentioned, the supreme Court shall have appellate Jurisdiction, both as to Law and Fact, with such Exceptions, and under such Regulations as the Congress shall make.

The Trial of all Crimes, except in Cases of Impeachment, shall be by Jury; and such Trial shall be held in the State where the said Crimes shall have been committed; but when not committed within any State, the Trial shall be at such Place or Places as the Congress may by Law have directed.

Section. 3.

Treason against the United States, shall consist only in levying War against them, or in adhering to their Enemies, giving them Aid and Comfort. No Person shall be convicted of Treason unless on the Testimony of two Witnesses to the same overt Act, or on Confession in open Court.

The Congress shall have Power to declare the Punishment of Treason, but no Attainder of Treason shall work Corruption of Blood, or Forfeiture except during the Life of the Person attainted.

Article. IV.

Section. 1.

Full Faith and Credit shall be given in each State to the public Acts, Records, and judicial Proceedings of every other State. And the Congress may by general Laws prescribe the Manner in which such Acts, Records and Proceedings shall be proved, and the Effect thereof.

Section. 2.

The Citizens of each State shall be entitled to all Privileges and Immunities of Citizens in the several States.

A Person charged in any State with Treason, Felony, or other Crime, who shall flee from Justice, and be found in another State, shall on Demand of the executive Authority of the State from which he fled, be delivered up, to be removed to the State having Jurisdiction of the Crime.

No Person held to Service or Labour in one State, under the Laws thereof, escaping into another, shall, in Consequence of any Law or Regulation therein, be discharged from such Service or Labour, but shall be delivered up on Claim of the Party to whom such Service or Labour may be due.

Section. 3.

New States may be admitted by the Congress into this Union; but no new State shall be formed or erected within the Jurisdiction of any other State; nor any State be formed by the Junction of two or more States, or Parts of States, without the Consent of the Legislatures of the States concerned as well as of the Congress.

The Congress shall have Power to dispose of and make all needful Rules and Regulations respecting the Territory or other Property belonging to the United States; and nothing in this Constitution shall be so construed as to Prejudice any Claims of the United States, or of any particular State.

Section. 4.

The United States shall guarantee to every State in this Union a Republican Form of Government, and shall protect each of them against Invasion; and on Application of the Legislature, or of the Executive (when the Legislature cannot be convened), against domestic Violence.

Article. V.

The Congress, whenever two thirds of both Houses shall deem it necessary, shall propose Amendments to this Constitution, or, on the Application of the Legislatures of two thirds of the several States, shall call a Convention for proposing Amendments, which, in either Case, shall be valid to all Intents and Purposes, as Part of this Constitution, when ratified by the Legislatures of three fourths of the several States, or by Conventions in three fourths thereof, as the one or the other Mode of Ratification may be proposed by the Congress; Provided that no Amendment which may be made prior to the Year One thousand eight hundred and eight shall in any Manner affect the first and fourth Clauses in the Ninth Section of the first Article; and that no State, without its Consent, shall be deprived of its equal Suffrage in the Senate.

Article. VI.

All Debts contracted and Engagements entered into, before the Adoption of this Constitution, shall be as valid against the United States under this Constitution, as under the Confederation.

This Constitution, and the Laws of the United States which shall be made in Pursuance thereof; and all Treaties made, or which shall be made, under the Authority of the United States, shall be the supreme Law of the Land; and the Judges in every State shall be bound thereby, any Thing in the Constitution or Laws of any State to the Contrary notwithstanding.

The Senators and Representatives before mentioned, and the Members of the several State Legislatures, and all executive and judicial Officers, both of the United States and of the several States, shall be bound by Oath or Affirmation, to support this Constitution; but no religious Test shall ever be required as a Qualification to any Office or public Trust under the United States.

Article. VII.

The Ratification of the Conventions of nine States, shall be sufficient for the Establishment of this Constitution between the States so ratifying the Same.

The Word, "the," being interlined between the seventh and eighth Lines of the first Page, The Word "Thirty" being partly written on an Erazure in the fifteenth Line of the first Page, The Words "is tried" being interlined between the thirty second and thirty third Lines of the first Page and the Word "the" being interlined between the forty third and forty fourth Lines of the second Page.

Attest William Jackson Secretary

done in Convention by the Unanimous Consent of the States present the Seventeenth Day of September in the Year of our Lord one thousand seven hundred and Eighty seven and of the Independance of the United States of America the Twelfth In witness whereof We have hereunto subscribed our Names,

G°. Washington

Presidt and deputy from Virginia

Delaware

Geo: Read
Gunning Bedford jun
John Dickinson
Richard Bassett
Jaco: Broom

Maryland

James McHenry
Dan of St Thos. Jenifer
Danl. Carroll

Virginia

John Blair
James Madison Jr.

North Carolina

Wm. Blount
Richd. Dobbs Spaight
Hu Williamson

South Carolina

J. Rutledge

Charles Cotesworth Pinckney
Charles Pinckney
Pierce Butler

Georgia

William Few
Abr Baldwin

New Hampshire

John Langdon
Nicholas Gilman

Massachusetts

Nathaniel Gorham
Rufus King

Connecticut

Wm. Saml. Johnson
Roger Sherman

New York

Alexander Hamilton

New Jersey

Wil: Livingston
David Brearley
Wm. Paterson
Jona: Dayton

Pensylvania

B Franklin
Thomas Mifflin
Robt. Morris
Geo. Clymer
Thos. FitzSimons
Jared Ingersoll
James Wilson
Gouv Morris

Appendix C

Jesus Sermon on the Mount of Olives

Matthew 24: 1-44

The Destruction of the Temple and Signs of the End Times

24 Jesus left the temple and was walking away when his disciples came up to him to call his attention to its buildings. **2** "Do you see all these things?" he asked. "Truly I tell you, not one stone here will be left on another; every one will be thrown down."

3 As Jesus was sitting on the Mount of Olives, the disciples came to him privately. "Tell us," they said, "when will this happen, and what will be the sign of your coming and of the end of the age?"

4 Jesus answered: "Watch out that no one deceives you. **5** For many will come in my name, claiming, 'I am the Messiah,' and will deceive many. **6** You will hear of wars and rumors of wars, but see to it that you are not alarmed. Such things must happen, but the end is still to come. ⁷ Nation will rise against nation, and kingdom against kingdom. There will be famines and earthquakes in various places. ⁸ All these are the beginning of birth pains.

⁹ "Then you will be handed over to be persecuted and put to death, and you will be hated by all nations because of me. ¹⁰ At that time many will turn away from the faith and will betray and hate each other, ¹¹ and many false prophets will appear and deceive many people. ¹² Because of the increase of wickedness, the love of most will grow cold, ¹³ but the one who stands firm to the end will be saved. ¹⁴ And this gospel of the kingdom will be preached in the whole world as a testimony to all nations, and then the end will come.

¹⁵ "So when you see standing in the holy place 'the abomination that causes desolation,'[a] spoken of through the prophet Daniel—let the reader understand— ¹⁶ then let those who are in Judea flee to the mountains. ¹⁷ Let no one on the housetop go down to take anything out of the house. ¹⁸ Let no one in the field go back to get their cloak. ¹⁹ How dreadful it will be in those days for pregnant women and nursing mothers! ²⁰ Pray that your flight will not take place in winter or on the Sabbath. ²¹ For then there will be great distress, unequaled from the beginning of the world until now—and never to be equaled again.

²² "If those days had not been cut short, no one would survive, but for the sake of the elect those days will be shortened. ²³ At that time if anyone says to you, 'Look, here is the Messiah!' or, 'There he is!' do not believe it. ²⁴ For false messiahs and false prophets will appear and perform great signs and wonders to deceive, if possible, even the elect. ²⁵ See, I have told you ahead of time.

²⁶ "So if anyone tells you, 'There he is, out in the wilderness,' do not go out; or, 'Here he is, in the inner rooms,' do not believe it. ²⁷ For as lightning that comes from the east is visible even in the west, so will be the coming of the Son of Man. ²⁸ Wherever there is a carcass, there the vultures will gather.

²⁹ "Immediately after the distress of those days' the sun will be darkened, and the moon will not give its light; the stars will fall from the sky, and the heavenly bodies will be shaken.'[b]

³⁰ "Then will appear the sign of the Son of Man in heaven. And then all the peoples of the earth[c] will mourn when they see the Son of Man coming on the clouds of heaven, with power and great glory. [d] ³¹ And he will send his angels with a loud trumpet call, and they will gather his elect from the four winds, from one end of the heavens to the other.

³² "Now learn this lesson from the fig tree: As soon as its twigs get tender and its leaves come out, you know that summer is near. ³³ Even so, when you see all these things, you know that it[e] is near, right at the door. ³⁴ Truly I tell you, this generation will certainly not pass away until all these things have happened. ³⁵ Heaven and earth will pass away, but my words will never pass away.

The Day and Hour Unknown

³⁶ "But about that day or hour no one knows, not even the angels in heaven, nor the Son,[f] but only the Father. ³⁷ As it was in the days of Noah, so it will be at the coming of the Son of Man. ³⁸ For in the days before the flood, people were eating and drinking, marrying and giving in marriage, up to the day Noah entered the ark; ³⁹ and they knew nothing about what would happen until the flood came and took them all away. That is how it will be at the coming of the Son of Man. ⁴⁰ Two men will be in the field; one will be taken and

the other left. [41] Two women will be grinding with a hand mill; one will be taken and the other left.

[42] "Therefore keep watch, because you do not know on what day your Lord will come. [43] But understand this: If the owner of the house had known at what time of night the thief was coming, he would have kept watch and would not have let his house be broken into. [44] So you also must be ready, because the Son of Man will come at an hour when you do not expect him.

Appendix D
Author's Other Writing

In Industry

1. "Manufacturing Planning Using Simulation", co-authored with Felipe K. Tan. It was published as part of the proceedings of the Annual Institute Conference and Convention of the American Institute of Industrial Engineers. It was presented in Toronto, Canada in April, 1967 at the conference.
2. "Computer Simulation in Action – Planning Maintenance Manpower Needs". It was published in the February 1970 issue of Computer Decisions magazine.
3. "Discrete Simulation – New Tool For Control and System Design". It was published as the feature article of the May 1970 issue of Control Engineering magazine.
4. "Maintenance Manpower Planning". It was published and presented in July 1971 as part of the Symposium on Computer Simulation as related to Manpower and Personnel Planning, sponsored by the Naval Personnel Research and Development Laboratory and held at the Naval Academy.

In Retirement

2003   Fulfilling an American Dream – for family

2007   Family History – for family

2012   Serving My Country in the U. S. Army – for family

2013   What Happened to My Hometown, Jamestown, N. Y.? –
       OPED printed in the Jamestown Post-Journal on June 16,
       2013

2013   A Way to Re-grow My hometown – OPED printed June
       30, 2013

2013   Response to OPED comments – submitted but not published

2014   1974 Six Week Burling Family Camping Trip Out West –
       for family

In process – The Endwell Connection – for family and friends

Appendix E

Blessings shared with congregation at a Temple Talk

1. Knowing that Jesus Christ is my personal savior. He died on the cross for all of my sins and in believing in Him, I will have eternal life
2. Being born in a country that has a Constitution that guarantees me freedom and protection of personal property; i. e. life, liberty and the pursuit of happiness
3. Being born to two loving parents that:
    a. Taught me about Jesus Christ and his message
    b. Brought me up in an atmosphere of love; for me, for each other and for others
    c. Taught me to be self reliant

4. Having met Joanne, a wonderful and caring person on a blind date on New Year's Eve, who I fell in love with and

have been married to for fifty five years and as a stay-at-home mom, took care of our children and our homes

5. Blessed with four beautiful children – two girls and two boys
6. Blessed with five beautiful grandchildren – one girl and four boys
7. Blessed with God given talent and health that I was able to provide for my family
8. Blessed with enough resources to have been retired over twenty five years and have been able to pursue most personal interests
9. Blessed to have a multitude of friends all over our country and many found relatives here and in Sweden through genealogy research
10. Blessed to have been able to travel all over our country, to England and to Sweden with all our children to attend a first time family reunion. It was held in the schoolhouse my father attended through the third grade when he had to quit to work on a farm to help support his family. It was the trip of our lifetime
11. Blessed to be a two time cancer survivor from 2002 and 2004.
12. Blessed to have had many reunions with our U. S. family to celebrate special occasions even as we live miles apart

Printed in the United States
By Bookmasters